Created and designed by the editorial staff of ORTHO BOOKS

Project Editor   Sally W. Smith
Writer and Food Stylist   Cynthia Scheer
Designer   James Stockton
Photographer   Michael Lamotte
Photographic Stylist   Sara Slavin

Ortho Books

Publisher
Robert L. Iacopi

Editorial Director
Min S. Yee

Managing Editor
Anne Coolman

Horticultural Editor
Michael D. Smith

Senior Editors
Kenneth R. Burke
Sally W. Smith

Production Manager
Laurie Sheldon

Horticulturists
Michael D. McKinley
Deni W. Stein

Production Assistant
Darcie S. Furlan

Editorial Assistants
Laurie A. Black
Anne D. Pederson
William F. Yusavage

National Sales Manager
Garry P. Wellman

Operations/Distribution
William T. Pletcher

Operations Assistant
Donna M. White

Administrative Assistant
Georgiann Wright

Address all inquiries to:
Ortho Books
Chevron Chemical Company
Consumer Products Division
575 Market Street
San Francisco, CA 94105

Chevron Chemical Company
575 Market Street, San Francisco, CA 94105

Acknowledgments

Assistant Designer
Karen Tucker

Copyediting
Editcetera
Berkeley, CA

Typography
Turner & Brown
Santa Rosa, CA

Color Separations
Colorscan
Mountain View, CA

Special thanks to

BIA Cordon Bleu
Belmont, CA

M & M Ferris
Corte Madera, CA

Naomi Gonzalez
San Jose, CA

Janet H. Johnson
Woodside, CA

Sue Fisher King
San Francisco, CA

Connie Nicholson
San Carlos, CA

Phil Quattrociocchi
S.F. International Cheese Imports
San Francisco, CA

Sebring Sales, Inc.
San Francisco, CA

Robert Steffy
San Francisco, CA

Sue Williams
San Jose, CA

Front Cover Photograph

The colorful stew of chicken and
young vegetables is Chicken Navarin
(the recipe is on page 71). Vegetables
are added in stages to be sure each
is cooked to tender-crisp perfection.

Back Cover Photographs

Some of the colorful and inviting
soups and stews you will find in the
pages ahead are:

Upper left: Creamy Pink Borsch,
page 29

Upper right: Fisherman's Wharf
Cioppino, page 75

Lower left: Lamb Meatball Irish Stew,
page 84

Lower right: Onion Soup with Beer,
page 14

Title Page

Home economist and writer Cynthia
Scheer can't resist a striking soup
tureen. This one bears a main dish
soup from Chapter 3.

Soup is such a universally understood food that it hardly needs defining. Indeed, the word finds its way into many sayings having nothing to do with eating. One gropes through a "pea-soup fog." Ordinary cars are outpaced by one with a "souped-up" engine. A troublesome situation has one "in the soup." Well-meaning meddlers are reminded that "too many cooks spoil the broth."

Stews are almost as much a part of everyday awareness. In addition to kitchen usage, we all know someone who "stews" over a vexing problem or, worse yet, is "left to stew in his own juices."

So many nonculinary uses of the words *soup* and *stew* have to do with troublesome situations that it may be better to return to the realm of the kettle and the wooden spoon where, instead, they offer a multitude of delicious opportunities. For that is the subject of this cookbook.

A very fine line separates the soup from the stew. It is probably a matter of liquid or, if you will, soupiness. The thicker the soup, the more likely it is to be considered a stew.

An ill-defined but much savored middle ground consists of dishes in which meats, poultry, or fish cook in an abundant broth. When all is ready, the flavor-packed broth is served as a first-course soup, followed by the meat or whatever as a main course.

Such dishes as French *bouillabaisse* and *petite marmite,* Italian *bollito misto,* and Austrian *Tafelspitz* are but a few examples of this sort of one-pot resourcefulness. They may be a problem to classify, but it is easy to appreciate them.

The heart of many of the soups and stews in this cookbook is a flavorsome homemade stock such as Sturdy Beef Broth (recipe, page 8).

Soup-Making Tools

Both soups and stews are such basic kinds of dishes that one hardly needs a sophisticated *batterie de cuisine* to do them justice. But experienced cooks find the following items helpful, and if you enjoy this kind of cooking, it will be useful to accumulate some or all of these utensils.

A *big, heavy stock pot* is essential for making your own broth. When you start with a quantity of bones, they take up a lot of room. The beef broth on page 8, for example, needs a kettle that holds at least 12 quarts; the chicken broth, an 8- to 10-quart one.

For most of the first-course soups in the second chapter, a *3-quart saucepan* is needed. Remember the rule of thumb that a heavier pan heats more evenly—but it should not be so heavy that it is hard for you to handle.

For the full-meal soups in the third chapter, a versatile pan is a *5- to 6-quart Dutch oven or deep kettle*. It will also be useful for many of the traditional stews in Chapter 4.

Many family stews (Chapter 5), a number of which can be quickly put together on top of the range, make good use of a *deep 10- to 12-inch frying pan with a cover*.

To strain out the bones and vegetables from homemade broth, you need two things: a *large colander* with fine perforations, to fit without spilling or tipping over a *great big bowl* that can withstand the high temperature of the hot broth.

For turning cooked vegetable mixtures into creamy, elegant purées, you will need a *blender or food processor*. Both do the job superbly, but the food processor also offers the convenience of grating, shredding, slicing, and chopping vegetables and other soup and stew ingredients. You can also use a hand-operated *food mill* to purée vegetables.

Saving Soups and Stews for a Rainy Day

Few foods freeze as easily or as well as soups and stews. Here are some ideas for freezing them at different stages during preparation, for convenience.

Freeze bones (beef, chicken, or whatever) in sealed, heavy plastic bags or packaged in freezer paper until you are ready to make broth.

Freeze broth in quantities you can use easily to make soups and stews. About 1 quart is a good amount for a first-course soup; measured 1- and 2-cup amounts are useful for stews. Use plastic or coated-cardboard freezer containers, coffee or shortening cans,

For a soup and stew cook's kitchen: a stock pot, large kettle, Dutch oven, covered frying pan, and other equipment, all described above.

or glass jars. Remember to leave about 1 inch of room at the top of the container to allow for expansion of the liquid as it freezes.

Freeze finished soups, ready to heat and serve. Mark them with the freezing date, because they should be used within 4 months. Reheat over direct low heat, stirring constantly, unless the soup contains milk; creamy soups should be reheated in a double boiler over simmering water.

A soup thickened with egg, such as the Danish Asparagus and Chicken Soup (page 24), may break down on reheating. If you wish to prepare such a soup ahead and freeze it, wait to add the egg until after the frozen soup is thawed and reheated.

Bright, fresh green vegetables that are added toward the end of cooking in recipes such as Minestrone Milanese (page 41) will be more appealing if you wait to add them until the frozen soup has been reheated

and is nearly ready to serve.

Freezing stews is somewhat trickier. The factor to look for is the thickening agent. If the stew is thickened simply by cooking it down until the liquid in it is of a substantial consistency—until it has enough body not to run all over the plate—then the stew can be frozen with no special precautions.

Stew thickened with flour or cornstarch may break down and separate after freezing. If you plan to freeze such a stew to serve later, substitute rice flour, tablespoon for tablespoon for flour, or two tablespoons to one for cornstarch.

Treat egg-thickened stews as you would an egg-thickened soup (see above).

As is the case for soups, if stews contain tender green vegetables, adding them after freezing and reheating will give the best color and texture.

Use frozen stews within 4 to 6 months.

Stock Up on Homemade Broth

The mainstay of a sturdy soup (or even a light, delicate one) is a well-made broth. It is not difficult to prepare your own beef, chicken, fish, or vegetable broth. You'll need a large pot, a mélange of flavorsome vegetables available the year around, and enough time to let the broth simmer until it becomes a delicious, full-bodied infusion of all that has gone into it. Fortunately, once the broth begins to cook gently, you can leave it alone for hours without attention.

Broth is more than the heart of a good soup. On its own, clarified beef or chicken broth (see pages 8–9) stars as sparkling consommé. Broth also makes a delicious liquid ingredient in many stews, sauces, and gravies. And you will treasure your homemade broth for turning rice into a perfect pilaf.

Garnishes to Dress Up Soups

No matter how good a bowl of plain soup tastes, something on top adds visual interest to entice the appetite. That something can be ever so simple: a dusting of nutmeg or freshly ground pepper, a few snips of chives or parsley, a single mushroom slice. A puréed vegetable or creamy soup takes well to a crunchy addition such as a tiny salted pretzel, a fish-shaped cracker, or the Garlic Croutons that follow. Clear soups can be enhanced by poached tiny meatballs or Danish Meat Dumplings, or by swirls of Parslied Pancake Strips, as a change from noodles.

Garlic Croutons

- 8 slices firm white or whole wheat bread
- 2 tablespoons *each* salad oil and butter or margarine
- 1 small clove garlic, minced or pressed
- ⅛ teaspoon paprika

1. Trim crusts from bread and discard them. Dice bread into ½-inch cubes.

2. In a large frying pan, combine oil and butter; place over medium heat until melted. Stir in garlic and paprika. Add bread, stirring until well coated.

3. Transfer bread cubes to a rimmed baking sheet and spread in a single layer. Bake in a 300°F oven until lightly browned and crisp (20 to 25 minutes). Cool; then store in a covered container in a cool place for up to 5 days, or freeze for longer storage.

Makes about 2½ cups.

Danish Meat Dumplings

- ½ pound cubed lean pork shoulder
- ¼ cup coarsely chopped onion
- 3 tablespoons all-purpose flour
- ½ teaspoon salt
  Pinch *each* white pepper and ground nutmeg
- 1 egg white
- ¼ to ⅓ cup milk
- 2 quarts salted water

1. In food processor with metal blade, combine pork, onion, flour, salt, pepper, nutmeg, and egg white. Process until pork is very finely chopped. Then add milk through feed tube, a little at a time, until mixture has consistency of cooked oatmeal.

2. In a 3-quart pan, bring salted water to boiling. Drop about half of the meat mixture by rounded teaspoons into water. As soon as the water returns to boiling, add a little cold water. Bring to boiling again, add a little more cold water to slow boiling, and repeat this process once more. Remove dumplings with a slotted spoon and drain

well. Repeat with remaining meat mixture.

3. If dumplings are made ahead, arrange them in a shallow pan in a single layer, cover, and refrigerate for up to 1 day. Add to hot soup to reheat.

Makes about 36 small dumplings.

Parslied Pancake Strips

- 1 egg
- ⅔ cup milk
- ½ cup all-purpose flour
- ⅛ teaspoon salt
- 2 tablespoons chopped fresh parsley
- 1 to 2 tablespoons butter or margarine

1. In blender or food processor, combine all ingredients except parsley and butter. Whirl or process until batter is smooth. Stir in parsley.

2. For each pancake, melt about ½ teaspoon of the butter in a 7- to 8-inch crêpe pan or frying pan over medium heat until bubbling. Add 2 to 3 tablespoons of the batter, tilting pan so batter covers bottom evenly. Cook until pancake is set and lightly browned on each side, turning once.

3. As soon as cooked pancake is cool enough to handle, roll it up tightly. When all are cooked, cut pancake rolls into ⅛- to ¼-inch strips.

Makes 2½ to 3 cups pancake strips.

Sturdy Beef Broth

Thanks to an abundance of bones, this broth is sturdy indeed. It contains so much natural gelatin that as it chills it becomes a quivery solid. That's the advantage of using this wonderful broth as the backbone of soups and stews—it gives their broth or gravy real substance.

As the broth cooks down, the flavor becomes quite concentrated, so it is best to wait to add salt until you use the stock. Otherwise you may find that a dish made with the stock has inadvertently become too salty.

8 to 10 pounds meaty beef bones

1 veal shank (1 to 1¼ lbs), cut across bone into 2-inch slices

3 medium carrots

3 large onions

2 stalks celery, with leaves, chopped

1 can (1 lb) tomatoes

Salt (optional)

1. Place bones in a large open roasting pan in a single layer. Top with one of the carrots (sliced) and one of the onions (thickly sliced). Bake in a 450°F oven, uncovered, until meat and bones are well browned (about 30 minutes).

2. Transfer the mixture to a large, deep kettle (at least 12-quart size). Add a little water to roasting pan, stirring to dissolve brown drippings; add to bone mixture in kettle. Add remaining carrots and onions (chopped), the celery, and the tomatoes (coarsely chopped) with their liquid. Add enough water to cover bones. Bring to boiling, cover, reduce heat, and simmer for 12 to 18 hours.

3. Strain the broth to remove bones and vegetables. Return the broth to cooking pot. Boil gently, uncovered, until it is reduced by about a fourth (30 to 45 minutes).

4. Moisten a large piece of cheesecloth or a clean muslin cloth; wring out thoroughly. Line a large colander with several thicknesses of cheesecloth or the muslin; place in a large bowl. Strain the broth through the cloth. Taste, and add salt if you wish. Cover and refrigerate broth for several hours or overnight.

5. Remove fat and discard. Place broth in 1- and 2-quart containers and seal tightly to store. Freeze; or cover and refrigerate, and use within 3 to 4 days.

Makes 2½ to 3 quarts.

Vegetarian Vegetable Broth draws its flavor from leeks, carrots, celery, onions, and herbs. Use it as a non-meat substitute for beef or chicken broth in most soups, or as the cooking liquid in any full-meal stew.

Rich Chicken Broth

Some swear by it as a cure-all. Others could not cook a week's worth of meals without using it at least once. Making your own chicken broth—especially if you buy whole chickens, cut them up yourself, and reserve the backs, necks, and wings until you have enough for a batch of broth—is a lot more economical than buying the canned kind.

- 1 medium onion, chopped
- 2 medium leeks, cleaned well and thinly sliced (use part of green tops)
- 1 large carrot, thinly sliced
- 1 stalk celery, with leaves, chopped
- 2 tablespoons butter or margarine
- 5 pounds bony chicken pieces (backs, necks, and/or wings)
- 3 sprigs parsley
- ¼ teaspoon *each* dried thyme and whole white or black peppercorns
- 1 bay leaf
  Pinch dried marjoram
- 4 quarts water
  Salt

1. In a large, deep kettle (8- to 10-quart size), cook onion, leeks, carrot, and celery in melted butter over medium heat, stirring often, until onions are soft but not brown. Add chicken pieces, parsley, thyme, peppercorns, bay leaf, marjoram, and water.

2. Bring slowly to boiling, reduce heat, cover, and simmer for 3½ to 4 hours, until broth has a rich flavor.

3. Strain the broth, discarding solids. Return broth to kettle and boil gently, uncovered, until it is reduced to about 3 quarts (30 minutes to 1 hour). Taste, and add salt if you wish.

4. If possible, refrigerate broth overnight; then skim off and discard fat. Freeze; or cover and refrigerate, and use within 3 to 4 days.

Makes about 3 quarts.

Vegetarian Vegetable Broth

This economical soup base tastes good and adds a lot to any soup of which it is a part. However, it lacks the intensity and stick-to-the-ribs quality of broth made with chicken or beef bones. You can use it as a substitute for chicken or beef broth in most recipes for puréed or cream soups or as the cooking liquid in any full-meal soup or stew.

- 2 large leeks (about 1½ lbs)
- 3 tablespoons butter or margarine
- 3 large carrots, chopped
- 3 stalks celery, with leaves, thinly sliced
- 2 large onions, chopped
- 1 clove garlic, slivered
- 3 quarts water
- 2 teaspoons salt
- 5 sprigs parsley
- 1 bay leaf
- 1 teaspoon dried thyme
- ¼ teaspoon whole black peppercorns

1. Cut off root ends of leeks; remove and discard coarse outer leaves. Cut off and discard coarse ends of green tops so that leeks are about 10 inches long. Split lengthwise, from leafy end, cutting to within about 1 inch of root end. Soak in cold water for several minutes, then separate leaves under running water to rinse away any grit; drain. Slice about ¼ inch thick.

2. Melt butter in an 8-quart kettle over medium heat. Add leeks, carrots, celery, onions, and garlic; cook, stirring often, until vegetables are soft but not brown (15 to 20 minutes).

3. Add water, salt, parsley, bay leaf, thyme, and peppercorns. Bring slowly to boiling; then cover, reduce heat, and simmer for 2 hours.

4. Strain broth, discarding solids. Cool; then freeze; or cover and refrigerate, and use within 3 to 4 days.

Makes about 2½ quarts.

Fish Broth

Many recipes for fish soups, chowders, and seafood stews that call for fish broth suggest bottled clam juice as a possible substitute. Broth is really better because it is more subtle—it gives a gentle marine flavor without obtrusive fishiness.

Most fish dealers will sell you fish scraps—heads and trimmings—for little or nothing. It is best to avoid fat-rich or oily fish when making this broth; that is why salmon is not recommended.

- 1 large onion, finely chopped
- 1 medium carrot, chopped
- 1 stalk celery, with leaves, thinly sliced
- ¼ cup butter or margarine
- 2 to 3 pounds fish bones and heads (no salmon)
- 8 sprigs parsley
- 1 teaspoon whole white peppercorns
- ¼ teaspoon dried thyme
- 1 bay leaf
- 2 cups dry white wine
- 1½ to 2 quarts water

1. In a deep 4- to 6-quart kettle, cook onion, carrot, and celery in melted butter over medium heat, stirring often, until onions are soft but not brown. Add fish, parsley, peppercorns, thyme, bay leaf, and wine. Pour in water to barely cover fish.

2. Bring slowly to boiling, reduce heat, cover, and simmer for 30 minutes.

3. Strain the broth, discarding solids. Taste broth, and if you wish to concentrate the flavor, boil it gently, uncovered, for 20 to 30 minutes more.

4. Freeze; or cover and refrigerate, and use within 2 days. Remove any solid fat from surface before using.

Makes 1½ to 2 quarts.

Clear Soups That Sparkle

Perhaps you believe, as did a character in a short story by Saki, that clear soup is "a more important factor in life than a clear conscience." If so, you may be dissatisfied with broth that has only been strained. Although you may strain broth carefully, even through cheesecloth or muslin, there are still enough suspended particles in it to make it somewhat cloudy.

Here is the way to transform homemade chicken or beef stock into sparkling clear broth.

1. Measure broth; use *2 egg whites* (¼ cup) for each *4 cups broth*. Beat egg whites until foamy.

2. Bring broth to boiling in a large pot. Whisking constantly, add egg whites to broth. Return to a full boil. Remove from heat and let stand to cool slightly.

3. Line a colander (placed over a large bowl) with a dampened, well-wrung-out muslin cloth. Slowly pour broth through cloth. Twist ends of cloth and gently press out liquid. Discard solids. Reheat broth and use at once, or refrigerate for up to 2 days.

THE LIGHT TOUCH IN SOUPS

"Soup's on!" In many families this cheery call means it's time to eat. The soups in this chapter are the sort to serve first, to open a formal dinner. But they are also appropriate for many other kinds of meals, at just about any time of the day.

Although these soups are on the light side, often you will find them just right with crackers or bread, cheese, a salad, or fruit for lunch or supper. Pack one of the soups in a thermos to take on a cool-weather picnic. Or tuck a small vacuum bottle of soup into a lunch box to add substance to a midday meal away from home.

Suggestions for building an entire meal around one spectacular dish include menus for an after-theater onion soup supper (pages 14–15); a winter lunch with a nippy Cheddar cheese soup (pages 18–19); a football buffet highlighted by an autumn squash soup (pages 20–21); and a Scandinavian dinner with an elegant fresh asparagus and chicken soup as its first course (pages 24–25).

Soup is something to appreciate the year around—steaming hot in chilly weather, frosty-cold in summer. And some, such as Sherried Artichoke Soup (page 27), are delicious either way.

To add interest to soups, consider the good-tasting garnishes on page 7. And for those who really love soup, why not soup for dessert or breakfast? The fruit soup recipes on page 30 offer some sweet surprises.

French Alpine Soup (see page 23 for the recipe) typifies the soups in this chapter, appropriate either for a first course or as part of a light repast.

Clear Soups

Sparkling broth is a classic dish. Additions of meat, poultry, or vegetables for flavor and color can be as simple or as complex as you choose. Canned stock or bouillon cubes and powders may be quick substitutes, but home-made broth (see pages 8–9) is clearly preferable. Keep it on hand in the freezer for soups such as these.

Danish Oxtail Consommé

This beautiful amber broth has its source in the humble but flavorful oxtail. Simmered slowly for rich flavor and then clarified expertly, it makes a subtly elegant first course with the addition of tiny meat dumplings, bits of carrot and leek, and a splash of Madeira.

2½ to 3 pounds oxtails, cut in segments

2 quarts water

2 medium carrots

1 large onion, chopped

1 clove garlic, slivered

¼ teaspoon *each* dried thyme and whole black peppercorns

3 sprigs parsley

1 bay leaf

2 tablespoons tomato paste

4 egg whites (about ½ cup)

1 medium leek

Salt (optional)

Danish Meat Dumplings (see page 7)

3 tablespoons Madeira or sherry

1. Place oxtails in a shallow baking pan in a single layer. Bake, uncovered, in a 450°F oven until meat is well browned (25 to 30 minutes).

2. Transfer oxtails to a deep 5- to 6-quart kettle. Add a little of the water to roasting pan, stirring to dissolve brown drippings. Add to oxtails. Chop 1 of the carrots and add to oxtails with onion, garlic, thyme, peppercorns, parsley, bay leaf, and tomato paste. Add remaining water. Bring to boiling, cover, reduce heat, and simmer until meat is very tender and broth is richly flavored (3 to 4 hours).

3. Strain the broth; discard solids, reserving meat for other uses if you wish. (This can be done ahead; refrigerate broth until ready to complete soup.) Skim and discard fat.

Spanish Garlic Soup makes a flavorful lunch with a cup of hot tea and fresh fruits.

4. Return the broth to a clean kettle. Bring to boiling and clarify with egg whites as directed on page 9. Strain as directed and return to a clean kettle. Reheat.

5. Cut remaining carrot lengthwise into quarters; then thinly slice crosswise. Cut off root end of leek; remove coarse outer leaves. Cut off and discard dark green top. Split leek lengthwise, from leafy end, cutting to within about 1 inch of root end. Soak in cold water for several minutes; then separate leaves under running water to rinse away any clinging grit. Drain and slice leek about ¼ inch thick.

6. Add vegetables to hot clarified broth and cook, covered, over medium heat, until vegetables are tender-crisp (about 5 minutes). Taste, and add salt if needed. Add Danish Meat Dumplings and heat through. Stir in Madeira and heat for about 1 minute longer. Serve hot.

Makes 6 servings (6 to 8 cups).

Double Mushroom Soup with Barley

Fresh ginger hints of the Orient in this easy soup combining fresh Japanese tree oyster mushrooms with the more familiar cultivated kind.

¼ cup butter or margarine

1 package (4 oz) fresh tree oyster or other Japanese-type mushrooms (small mushrooms whole and larger ones slivered)

¼ pound cultivated mushrooms, thinly sliced

¼ cup pearl barley, rinsed and drained

1 small clove garlic, minced or pressed

3½ cups Sturdy Beef Broth (see page 8) *or* 2 cans (14½ oz *each*) regular-strength beef broth

1 teaspoon grated fresh ginger *or* ¼ teaspoon ground ginger

Salt and white pepper

2 green onions, thinly sliced on the diagonal

1. Melt butter in a heavy 2- to 3-quart saucepan over medium heat. Add both kinds of mushrooms and cook, stirring occasionally, until they are lightly browned and any liquid has cooked away. Add barley and garlic, stirring to coat barley with mushroom mixture.

2. Mix in 1 cup of the broth. Bring to boiling, cover, reduce heat, and simmer until barley is tender (about 45 minutes).

3. Mix in ginger and remaining 2½ cups of the broth. Cook, uncovered, over medium heat until soup is steaming hot. Taste, and add salt if needed; add pepper to taste. Just before serving, stir in onions.

Makes 4 servings (4 cups).

THE LIGHT TOUCH IN SOUPS

Spanish Garlic Soup

Poached eggs and bacon enrich this pungently flavored broth. You can serve the soup as the first course of a light dinner with grilled chicken or fish or as a lunch dish with fresh fruit.

- **3 thick slices bacon, cut crosswise in thin strips**
- **3 tablespoons olive oil**
- **8 cloves garlic, sliced**
- **1 tablespoon tomato paste**
- **3½ cups Sturdy Beef Broth (see page 8) *or* 2 cans (14½ oz each) beef broth**
- **½ cup dry sherry**
- **Salt and pepper**
- **Baguette Croutons (recipe follows)**
- **Poached Eggs (directions follow)**
- **Fresh cilantro (Chinese parsley) or parsley leaves (optional)**

1. In a heavy 2- to 3-quart saucepan, cook bacon until crisp and golden brown. Remove bacon pieces with a slotted spoon and drain on paper towels. Discard bacon drippings.

2. In same pan, heat olive oil over medium heat. Add garlic and cook, stirring often, until lightly browned. Meanwhile, dilute tomato paste with a little of the broth; then add both remaining broth and diluted tomato paste to garlic mixture. Bring to boiling, cover, reduce heat, and simmer for 20 minutes.

3. Remove garlic from broth with a slotted spoon; discard garlic. Add sherry to broth. Season with salt and pepper to taste. Reheat until broth begins to boil.

4. To serve, divide hot Baguette Croutons among warm soup bowls. Put a poached egg into each bowl on top of croutons. Pour steaming hot soup over eggs and let stand for about half a minute before serving. Sprinkle each serving with bacon, and with cilantro or parsley if you wish.

Makes 4 servings (4½ to 5 cups).

Baguette Croutons Cut eight ¼-inch-thick slices from a long, thin loaf of French bread. Arrange in a single layer on a baking sheet. Melt 1 tablespoon butter or margarine with 1 teaspoon olive oil and a pinch of cayenne pepper; brush butter mixture evenly over bread slices. Bake in a 300°F oven until crisp and lightly browned (20 to 25 minutes). Reheat, if necessary, just before serving in soup. Makes 8 croutons.

Poached Eggs Immerse 4 eggs (in shells) in rapidly boiling water for 5 seconds; remove eggs and set them aside. Pour water into a large, deep frying pan to a depth of about 2½ inches; place over high heat until water begins to boil. Then adjust heat so that water barely bubbles. Break eggs directly into water and cook gently until whites are firm (2 to 3 minutes). Remove poached eggs from cooking water with a slotted spoon and serve at once, or immerse them in a bowl of very cold water. If cooked ahead, cover and refrigerate; to reheat eggs, transfer to a bowl of water that is just hot to the touch and let stand 5 to 10 minutes. Just before serving transfer eggs to soup bowls as directed in recipe.

Taxco Miners' Soup

Hot, crisply fried tortilla strips sizzle as this zesty Mexican soup is ladled over them. After the soup, serve grilled snapper or shrimp with garlic butter, and a green vegetable.

- **Salad oil for frying**
- **4 corn tortillas (6-in. diam), cut in halves, then into ½-inch-wide strips**
- **Salt**
- **1 tablespoon olive oil or salad oil**
- **1 medium onion, thinly slivered**
- **1 small clove garlic, minced or pressed**
- **½ teaspoon ground cumin**
- **2 canned green chiles, finely chopped**
- **1 large can (15 oz) tomato sauce**
- **2 cups Rich Chicken Broth (see page 9) *or* 1 can (14½ oz) chicken broth**
- **1 cup water**
- **¼ pound Monterey jack cheese, cut in ½-inch cubes (about 1 cup)**
- **Sour cream, for garnish (optional)**

1. Pour salad oil into a deep, heavy frying pan to a depth of about ½ inch. Heat to a temperature of 350° to 375°F. Fry tortilla strips, about a third at a time, until crisp and lightly browned (about 2 minutes). Remove with a slotted spoon to paper towels to drain. Salt lightly.

2. Heat the tablespoon of olive oil in a 2- to 3-quart saucepan over medium heat. Add onion and cook, stirring, until soft but not browned. Mix in garlic and cumin; then add green chiles, tomato sauce, broth, and water. Bring to boiling, cover, reduce heat, and simmer for 10 minutes.

3. Meanwhile, spread tortilla strips in a shallow pan and heat in a 325°F oven for 8 to 10 minutes. Place heatproof soup bowls on a baking sheet in same oven during last 5 minutes.

4. With potholders, remove hot soup bowls to a heatproof tray. Working quickly, divide hot tortilla strips among the bowls. Top with cheese cubes. Ladle hot soup over tortillas and cheese and serve at once.

5. Spoon in sour cream at the table if you wish.

Makes 4 servings (6 to 8 cups).

Serve a Mexican meal of Taxco Miners' Soup followed by grilled fish.

Beefy Red Wine and Tomato Soup

Noodlelike strips of parsley-flavored pancakes are an intriguing addition to this easy first-course soup.

3½ cups Sturdy Beef Broth (see page 8) or 2 cans (14½ oz each) beef broth

2 medium tomatoes, peeled, seeded, and chopped

1 tablespoon lemon juice

Parslied Pancake Strips (see page 7)

½ cup dry red wine

Salt and pepper

1. In a 2- to 3-quart enamel saucepan, combine broth, tomatoes, and lemon juice. Bring to boiling over medium heat; then cover, reduce heat, and simmer for 25 minutes. Meanwhile, make pancake strips.

2. Gradually stir red wine into soup. Reheat until steaming hot. Taste, and add salt and pepper as needed.

3. Divide pancake strips among 4 or 5 soup bowls. Add hot soup.

Makes 4 to 5 servings (5½ cups).

Chicken Soup with Lentils

Lentil soup is usually a hearty, stick-to-the-ribs affair. This version is not so filling.

2 tablespoons butter or margarine

1 small onion, thinly slivered

¼ cup each finely chopped celery and fresh parsley

1 medium carrot, shredded

½ cup dried lentils, rinsed and drained

⅛ teaspoon white pepper

Pinch ground cloves

5 cups Rich Chicken Broth (see page 9) or 3 cans (14½ oz each) chicken broth

Salt (optional)

1. In a 2- to 3-quart saucepan, melt butter over medium heat. Add onion, celery, parsley, and carrot. Cook, stirring often, until soft but not browned. Add lentils, pepper, cloves, and broth.

2. Bring to boiling, cover, reduce heat, and boil gently until lentils are tender (25 to 30 minutes).

3. Taste, and add salt if needed.

Makes 4 to 6 servings (about 6 cups).

Late Evening Soup Supper

Onion Soup with Beer

Dilled Lettuce, Tomato, and Cucumber Salad

Mocha-Almond Ice Cream Pie

Beer or Red Jug Wine   Coffee

When you come home hungry after the theater, a film, or an evening sporting event, this is the soup to have waiting. Crusty with thick slices of bread and cheese, it is a welcoming treat with a side dish of green salad and a glass of beer or red wine. If you crave a dessert, have the ice cream pie ready in the freezer.

To prepare the supper in advance, complete the soup through Step 3; shred and refrigerate the Swiss cheese. When you're ready to serve, add the remaining broth, reheat, and broil the soup in individual bowls with the topping. The salad ingredients and dressing can be prepared ahead; combine them just before serving.

Onion Soup with Beer

6 medium onions (2 to 2½ lbs)

⅓ cup butter or margarine

2 cloves garlic

3 tablespoons all-purpose flour

1 teaspoon paprika

1 bottle or can (12 oz) dark beer

2 quarts Sturdy Beef Broth (see page 8) or canned regular-strength beef broth

6 to 8 slices French bread, cut about 1 inch thick

6 to 8 tablespoons grated Parmesan cheese

Salt and pepper

2 to 3 cups (½ to ¾ lb) shredded Swiss cheese

1. Cut onions in half lengthwise, then into lengthwise slivers. Melt butter over medium heat in a 5- to 6-quart kettle. Add onions, cover, and cook until limp (about 10 minutes). Uncover and cook, stirring often, until onions brown lightly (about 15 minutes). Reduce heat to medium-low if onions begin to brown too quickly.

2. Mince or press 1 of the garlic cloves. Add the minced garlic, flour, and paprika to onions, stirring to blend flour into mixture. Remove from heat and gradually stir in beer and 2 cups of the broth. Return to heat and bring to boiling, stirring. Cover, reduce heat, and simmer for 1 hour.

3. Meanwhile, place bread slices on a baking sheet. Peel remaining clove of garlic, cut it in half, and with it rub both sides of each bread slice. Bake in a 325°F oven until crisp and lightly browned (40 to 45 minutes). Sprinkle each slice with 1 tablespoon of the Parmesan cheese.

4. After soup has simmered for 1 hour, add remaining 6 cups broth and bring it to a gentle boil. Season to taste.

5. Divide soup among ovenproof bowls. Top each with a slice of toasted French bread. Divide Swiss cheese evenly among the slices. Place bowls on a baking sheet about 6 inches below broiler. Broil until cheese is bubbling and lightly browned (6 to 8 minutes). Serve at once.

Makes 6 to 8 servings (10 to 12 cups).

Dilled Lettuce, Tomato, and Cucumber Salad

1 small cucumber

10 cups torn butter or Boston lettuce

1 cup cherry tomatoes, cut in halves

Dill Dressing (recipe follows)

1. Peel cucumber, cut in half lengthwise, and scoop out and discard seeds. Slice thinly.

2. In a large salad bowl, combine cucumber, lettuce, and tomatoes.

3. Mix lightly with dressing.

Makes 6 to 8 servings.

Bubbly from the broiler, onion soup stars at a late supper after a night at the opera. The soup contains beer, which also tastes good with it.

Dill Dressing In a medium bowl, mix 2 tablespoons white wine vinegar, 2 teaspoons lemon juice, 1½ teaspoons Dijon mustard, 1 clove garlic (minced or pressed), ½ teaspoon dried dill-weed, ⅛ teaspoon salt, and a pinch of coarsely ground black pepper. Using a whisk or fork, gradually mix in 2 tablespoons olive oil and ⅓ cup salad oil until blended and slightly thickened. Makes about ½ cup.

Mocha-Almond Ice Cream Pie

Chocolate Chip Crust (recipe follows)

½ **cup** *each* **toasted slivered almonds and firmly packed brown sugar**

2 **tablespoons butter or margarine, melted**

½ **cup coarsely chopped semisweet chocolate**

1 **quart coffee ice cream, softened**

1 **teaspoon salad oil**

1. Bake crust in a 375°F oven until lightly browned (12 to 14 minutes). Cool in pan on a wire rack.

2. In a medium bowl, mix almonds, brown sugar, and butter. Add ¼ cup of the chopped chocolate and mix lightly.

3. Spread half of the ice cream in cooled crust. Sprinkle evenly with half of the almond mixture. Cover with remaining ice cream, then remaining almond mixture. Place in freezer.

4. Place remaining ¼ cup chopped chocolate over hot (but not boiling) water until melted. Stir in salad oil. Drizzle over top of partially frozen pie,

dribbling it from a spoon or using a cone of rolled paper to pipe it on. Return pie to freezer.

5. When top is set, cover with foil. Freeze until firm (3 to 4 hours or overnight).

6. Remove pie from freezer and let stand in refrigerator for about 30 minutes before cutting.

Makes 6 to 8 servings.

Chocolate Chip Crust Combine ⅓ cup butter or margarine (softened) and ¼ cup firmly packed brown sugar in a medium bowl; beat until fluffy. Beat in ½ teaspoon vanilla, then 1 egg yolk. Gradually blend in 1 cup all-purpose flour until mixture is combined. Blend in ¼ cup finely chopped semisweet chocolate. Press mixture evenly and firmly over bottom and up sides of a 9-inch pie pan. Pierce bottom in several places with a fork.

Puréed Soups

When you cook vegetables in broth and then whirl them in a blender or food processor, the result is a smooth, naturally thickened soup. Such soups have an inherent elegance as first courses. Most are complemented by a topping of buttery homemade croutons (see page 7).

Red Pepper Soup

You will enjoy the distinctive flavor of sweet red peppers in this soup, as well as its brilliant scarlet color.

3 large sweet red bell peppers (about 1¼ lbs), seeded and chopped

1 medium onion, finely chopped

3 tablespoons butter or margarine

¼ teaspoon ground cumin

Pinch cayenne pepper

3½ cups Rich Chicken Broth (see page 9) *or* **2 cans (14½ oz** *each***) chicken broth**

2 teaspoons lemon juice

Salt (optional)

Sweet red peppers, often used to accent salads, stews, and vegetable dishes, stand on their own in this colorful winter soup. Easily prepared in a little over half an hour, the soup consists of chopped peppers sautéed with onion in butter, cooked in broth, then puréed.

Few sprigs Italian (flat-leaf) parsley, for garnish

1. Cook peppers and onion in butter in a 3-quart saucepan over medium heat, stirring occasionally, until onion is soft but not browned. Mix in cumin and cayenne; then add chicken broth.

2. Bring to boiling, cover, reduce heat, and simmer for 20 minutes.

3. With a slotted spoon, scoop out vegetables and transfer to a blender or food processor. Add a little of the broth and whirl or process until smooth. Return red pepper purée to broth in cooking pan. Mix in lemon juice. Taste, and add salt if needed.

4. Reheat to serving temperature. Serve hot, garnishing each serving with a few leaves of parsley.

Makes 4 to 5 servings (5½ cups).

Basil and Spinach Soup with Lemon Cream

Fresh basil is the flavor secret of this soup finished with a dollop of lemony whipped cream.

2 bunches (about 1½ lbs) spinach

1 medium onion, finely chopped

3 tablespoons olive oil

1 clove garlic, minced or pressed

1 cup lightly packed fresh basil leaves

3½ cups Rich Chicken Broth (see page 9) *or* **2 cans (14½ oz each) chicken broth**

½ cup grated Parmesan cheese

1 cup whipping cream

Salt (optional)

2 teaspoons lemon juice

¼ teaspoon grated lemon peel

1. Rinse spinach well; drain; then remove and discard stems. (You should have about 4 quarts leaves, lightly packed.)

2. Cook onion in olive oil in a 4- to 5-quart kettle over medium heat until soft but not browned. Mix in garlic. Then add spinach and basil leaves, stirring often until leaves wilt.

3. Add broth. Bring to boiling, reduce heat, and simmer, uncovered, for 10 minutes.

4. With a slotted spoon, scoop out spinach and basil and transfer to a

blender or food processor. Add a little of the broth and whirl or process until smooth. Return purée to pan.

5. Mix in cheese and ⅔ cup of the whipping cream. Reheat to serving temperature; add salt if needed.

6. In a medium bowl, combine remaining ⅓ cup cream, lemon juice, and lemon peel. Beat until stiff. Spoon a little of the lemon cream over each serving of the hot soup.

Makes 4 to 6 servings (about 7 cups).

Orange and Tomato Soup

Orange peel and juice accent an easy-to-make tomato soup from the Chelsea section of London. Follow the soup with broiled lamb chops, broccoli, and a crusty gratin of potatoes.

1 medium onion, finely chopped

2 tablespoons butter or margarine

1 small clove garlic, minced or pressed

¼ teaspoon ground cumin

⅛ teaspoon white pepper

1 large can (28 oz) tomatoes

Grated peel and juice of 1 large orange

1¾ cups Rich Chicken Broth (see page 9) *or* **1 can (14½ oz) chicken broth**

Salt (optional)

Sour cream and additional grated orange peel, for garnish

1. Cook onion in butter in a 3- to 4-quart saucepan over medium heat until soft but not browned. Mix in garlic, cumin, and pepper. Then add tomatoes (break up with a fork) and their liquid. Mix in orange peel and juice and chicken broth.

2. Bring to boiling, cover, reduce heat, and simmer for 30 minutes.

3. Whirl or process soup, about half at a time, in a blender or food processor until smooth. Return purée to cooking pan; add salt if needed.

4. Reheat to serving temperature. Serve hot, garnishing each serving with a dollop of sour cream and a sprinkling of orange peel.

Makes 4 to 6 servings (6½ cups).

Sherried Black Bean Soup

An assortment of toppings—green onions, bacon, sour cream, hard-cooked eggs, and lemon slices—allows each guest to accent this suave bean soup to taste.

1 pound (about 2½ cups) dried black beans, rinsed and drained

2 quarts water

2 medium onions, chopped

1 stalk celery, thinly sliced

1 medium carrot, shredded

1 clove garlic, minced or pressed

2 tablespoons butter or margarine

1 ham hock (about 1 lb)

¼ cup chopped fresh parsley

1 teaspoon salt

⅛ teaspoon *each* **cayenne pepper, whole cloves, and mustard seed**

1 bay leaf

⅓ cup dry sherry

Thinly sliced green onions, crumbled crisp bacon, sour cream, sieved hard-cooked egg, and thin lemon slices, for garnish

1. Bring beans and 1 quart of the water to boiling in a large, heavy saucepan. Boil briskly for 2 minutes; then remove from heat and let stand, covered, for 1 hour.

2. Cook onions, celery, carrot, and garlic in butter in a 5-quart Dutch oven until soft but not browned. Add ham hock, remaining 1 quart water, parsley, salt, cayenne, cloves, mustard seed, bay leaf, and beans (with their liquid). Bring to boiling, cover, reduce heat, and simmer until ham and beans are tender (about 3 hours).

3. Remove ham hock and let cool slightly. Remove and discard bay leaf. Place about half of the beans with about 1 cup of the liquid from the soup in a blender or food processor. Whirl or process until smooth. Return purée to soup in Dutch oven.

4. Remove ham from bone and add meat to soup. (Discard fat, bones, and skin.) Reheat soup over medium heat until steaming hot. Mix in sherry. Taste, and add salt if needed.

5. Serve hot soup with choice of garnishes to sprinkle over each serving.

Makes 8 servings (8 to 10 cups).

Creamy Soups

Adding milk, half-and-half, or cream to a puréed soup changes its character considerably. Not only does the soup become silkier and seem more special, its nutritional profile also expands with the addition of protein and calcium. Though still in the first-course category, such soups can be offered in smaller servings in keeping with their increased richness.

French Cream of Mushroom Soup

Thick, and savory with herbs, this fresh mushroom soup will lure you away from its pallid canned counterpart forever.

- ¼ cup butter or margarine
- 1 pound mushrooms, thinly sliced
- 2 shallots, finely chopped (about ¼ cup)
- 1 tablespoon all-purpose flour
- ½ teaspoon *each* salt and dried savory
- Pinch white pepper
- 2 teaspoons tomato paste
- 2 cups Sturdy Beef Broth (see page 8) *or* 1 can (14½ oz) beef broth
- 1 tablespoon lemon juice
- 2 cups half-and-half (light cream)
- 2 tablespoons dry vermouth

1. In a 3-quart pan, melt butter over moderately high heat; add mushrooms and shallots; and cook, stirring often, until mushrooms brown lightly and most of their liquid is gone.

2. Sprinkle with flour, salt, savory, and pepper. Add tomato paste; stir mushrooms to coat with added ingredients. Remove from heat and gradually blend in beef broth. Bring to boiling, cover, reduce heat, and simmer for 20 minutes.

3. Purée mushroom mixture in blender or food processor until smooth, mixing in lemon juice at end. Return to cooking pan, blend in half-and-half, and stir often over medium heat until steaming hot. (Do not boil.) Taste, and add salt if needed.

4. Blend in vermouth and serve at once.

Makes 4 servings (about 5 cups).

Cream of Filbert Soup

If you love the flavor of toasted nuts, this creamy beige soup is for you.

- 1½ cups filberts
- ¼ cup butter or margarine
- 1 leek, thinly sliced (use pale green part of top only)
- 1 stalk celery, thinly sliced
- ¼ cup thinly sliced carrot
- 1 small clove garlic, minced or pressed
- Half a bay leaf
- 1 tablespoon all-purpose flour
- ½ teaspoon salt
- Pinch *each* ground nutmeg and white pepper
- 3½ cups Rich Chicken Broth (see page 9) *or* 2 cans (14½ oz each) chicken broth
- 1½ cups half-and-half (light cream)
- 2 tablespoons brandy

1. Spread filberts in a large, shallow pan and bake in a 350°F oven until lightly browned (8 to 10 minutes). Let stand until cool enough to handle; with fingers, rub off as much as possible of the skins. Discard skins.

2. In a 3-quart saucepan, melt butter over medium heat. Add leek, celery, carrot, and garlic; cook, stirring often, until vegetables are soft but not browned. Mix in bay leaf and filberts, then flour, salt, nutmeg, and pepper. Stir until well combined and bubbling.

3. Gradually blend in broth. Cook, stirring often, until mixture boils. Reduce heat, cover, and simmer for 20 minutes. ·

4. Remove and discard bay leaf. Whirl filbert mixture, about half at a time, in blender or food processor until smooth. Return to pan and blend in half-and-half. Cook, stirring often, until steaming hot. (Do not boil.) Taste, and add salt if needed.

5. Mix in brandy and serve at once.

Makes 6 servings (about 7 cups).

Chilly Day Lunch

Alehouse Cheese Soup

Greens and Apple Salad

Whole Wheat Bread   Butter

Grapes   Plump Ginger Cookies

Tea

Cheese and apples are favorite flavor partners. For this lunch, the cheese is in the golden soup, and the apples accent the accompanying salad.

Alehouse Cheese Soup

- 3 tablespoons butter or margarine
- 1 medium onion, chopped
- 2 stalks celery, thinly sliced
- 2 medium carrots, shredded
- 1 bottle or can (12 oz) dark beer
- 1¾ cups Rich Chicken Broth (see page 9) *or* 1 can (14½ oz) chicken broth
- 1 cup half-and-half (light cream)
- ⅛ teaspoon ground nutmeg
- 3 cups (¾ lb) shredded sharp Cheddar cheese
- Salt and cayenne pepper

1. In a 3-quart saucepan, melt butter over medium heat; add onion, celery, and carrots. Cook, stirring often, until onion is soft but not browned. Add beer and chicken broth. Bring to boiling, cover, reduce heat, and simmer until vegetables are very tender (about 20 minutes).

2. Transfer mixture to a blender or food processor; whirl or process until smooth. Return to pan and add half-and-half and nutmeg. Heat over medium-low heat, stirring occasionally, until soup is steaming.

3. Add cheese, about 2 tablespoons at a time, whisking after each addition until cheese melts. (Do not let soup boil.) Season to taste with salt and cayenne. Serve at once.

Makes 4 to 6 servings (about 7 cups).

Greens and Apple Salad

1 quart *each* torn romaine and red leaf lettuce

2 small tart green apples, cored and thinly sliced (unpeeled)

Creamy Tarragon Dressing (recipe follows)

⅓ cup coarsely chopped smoke-flavored almonds

1. In a large bowl, combine greens and apples.

2. Mix lightly with dressing.

3. Sprinkle with almonds and serve at once.

Makes 6 servings.

Creamy Tarragon Dressing In a medium bowl, mix 1 egg yolk, 1 tablespoon tarragon wine vinegar, 1½ teaspoons Dijon mustard, ⅛ teaspoon dried tarragon, a pinch of white pepper, and 1 shallot (finely chopped). Using a whisk or fork, slowly and gradually beat in ⅓ cup salad oil until dressing is thick and creamy. Makes about ½ cup.

Plump Ginger Cookies

¾ cup butter or margarine, softened

1 cup firmly packed brown sugar

1 egg

¼ cup light molasses

2¼ cups all-purpose flour

½ cup ground walnuts

1¾ teaspoons baking soda

⅛ teaspoon salt

1 teaspoon *each* ground ginger and cinnamon

½ teaspoon ground cloves

Granulated sugar

3 to 4 tablespoons red currant jelly

1. In a large bowl, cream butter and brown sugar until light and fluffy. Beat in egg, then molasses.

2. In a medium bowl, stir together flour, walnuts, baking soda, salt, ginger, cinnamon, and cloves.

3. Gradually add flour mixture to butter mixture, mixing until well blended. Drop batter by heaping tablespoons into granulated sugar in a shallow bowl. Roll each to form a ball, coating evenly with sugar. Place well apart on ungreased baking sheets.

4. With your finger or a small spoon, make a small, deep depression in center of each cookie; fill with currant jelly, using a rounded ¼ teaspoon for each.

5. Bake cookies in a 350°F oven until browned (15 to 18 minutes).

Makes 2 to 2½ dozen 2½-inch cookies.

Reminiscent of a Welsh rabbit, this soup is tangy with Cheddar cheese and beer—perfect for a winter lunch with a crisp apple salad.

Cheddar-Cauliflower Soup

A creamy cauliflower soup gilded with a touch of Cheddar cheese makes a hearty first course or a sturdy lunch or supper with bacon, lettuce, and tomato sandwiches.

1 small cauliflower (1¼ to 1½ lbs)

1 small onion, thinly sliced

½ teaspoon dried chervil or parsley

1¾ cups Rich Chicken Broth (see page 9) *or* 1 can (14½ oz) chicken broth

2 tablespoons butter or margarine

1 tablespoon all-purpose flour

¾ teaspoon salt

Pinch *each* ground nutmeg and white pepper

2 cups half-and-half (light cream)

1 cup (¼ lb) shredded sharp Cheddar cheese

1. Cut out and discard cauliflower core, remove and discard coarse outer leaves, and separate cauliflower into small flowerets. (You should have about 4 cups.)

2. In a 3-quart saucepan, combine cauliflower, onion, chervil, and broth. Bring to boiling, cover, reduce heat, and simmer until cauliflower is tender (10 to 12 minutes). Remove and reserve about a third of the cauliflower.

3. Transfer remaining cauliflower mixture to blender or food processor. Whirl or process until smooth.

4. In a 3- to 4-quart saucepan, melt butter over medium heat; stir in flour, salt, nutmeg, and pepper. Cook, stirring, until bubbly. Remove from heat and gradually blend in half-and-half. Return to heat and cook, stirring constantly, until mixture boils. Blend in cauliflower purée and ¾ cup of the cheese. Heat, stirring often, until soup is steaming and cheese melts.

5. Add reserved cauliflower and cook just until heated through (2 to 3 minutes). Serve sprinkled with remaining ¼ cup cheese.

Makes 5 to 6 servings (about 6 cups).

Football Buffet

Golden Squash Soup

Open-Faced Ham Sandwiches on Braided Oatmeal Bread

Bread-and-Butter Pickles

Radishes and Celery Sticks

Spicy Apple Upside-Down Cake

Beer or Cider   Coffee

Before or after the game, offer this buffet as lunch or supper. With bowls or mugs of the spirited soup, arrange sandwich makings for each guest to assemble: homemade bread, thinly sliced Westphalian or baked ham, lettuce, and mayonnaise or a seasoned butter (add a little horseradish and Dijon mustard to softened butter) in a small crock.

The bread recipe produces two loaves—one for this menu and a second to freeze for another occasion. The soup can be made through Step 2, covered, and refrigerated; to complete it, stir in the milk and heat to serving temperature. The cake is best served warm. If it is baked in advance, cover it lightly with foil and reheat in a 325°F oven for 15 to 20 minutes.

Golden Squash Soup

A 1½-pound piece winter squash

2 tablespoons butter or margarine

1 small onion, finely chopped

1 tablespoon all-purpose flour

2 tablespoons peanut butter

2 cups Rich Chicken Broth (see page 9) *or* 1 can (14½ oz) chicken broth

½ teaspoon *each* salt and dry mustard

Pinch *each* white pepper and cayenne pepper

2 cups milk

Sour cream, for garnish

1. To cook squash, place cut side down in a greased baking dish. Cover and bake in a 400°F oven until very tender (40 to 50 minutes). Scoop out squash and discard rind. (You should have about 2 cups cooked squash.) Purée in a blender or food processor or press through a food mill.

2. Melt butter in a 3-quart saucepan. Add onion and cook over medium heat until soft but not browned. Blend in flour, then peanut butter. Remove from heat and gradually blend in chicken broth. Blend in puréed squash, salt, dry mustard, pepper, and cayenne. Cook, stirring, until mixture thickens and boils.

3. Blend in milk and heat to serving temperature. Serve topped with dollops of sour cream.

Makes 4 to 6 servings (6 to 7 cups).

Braided Oatmeal Bread

1 cup rolled oats

1 cup boiling water

1 cup milk

3 tablespoons butter or margarine

¼ cup honey

2 teaspoons salt

1 envelope active dry yeast

¼ cup warm water

4½ to 5 cups unbleached all-purpose flour

1 cup wheat germ

1 egg yolk, beaten with 1 teaspoon water

2 tablespoons rolled oats

1. Place the 1 cup rolled oats in a medium bowl, pour on the boiling water, and let stand until mixture is lukewarm.

2. Scald milk in a small pan; remove from heat and add butter, honey, and salt. Stir until butter melts.

3. Sprinkle yeast over the warm water in the large bowl of an electric mixer; let stand until soft (about 5

You don't have to be a football fan to enjoy this sporty meal of zesty squash soup, sandwiches on homemade bread, and apple cake.

minutes). To yeast mixture add cooled oatmeal mixture, milk mixture, and 3 cups of the flour. Mix to blend; then beat at medium speed until smooth and elastic (about 5 minutes). Stir in wheat germ and about 1 cup more flour to make a stiff dough.

4. Turn dough out onto a board or pastry cloth floured generously with some of the remaining ½ to 1 cup flour. Knead until dough is smooth and springy and small bubbles form just under the surface, adding more flour to prevent dough from being too sticky (10 to 15 minutes).

5. Turn dough in a greased bowl. Cover and let rise in a warm place until doubled (1 to 1½ hours). Punch dough down and divide it in half. Divide each portion into 3 pieces.

6. On a lightly floured surface, roll each piece to a 15-inch-long strand. Place 3 strands side by side and braid, being careful not to stretch dough. Pinch ends to seal. Repeat with remaining 3 strands. Place each braid in a greased 4½- by 8½-inch loaf pan. Cover lightly and let rise until almost doubled (45 minutes to 1 hour). Brush egg mixture lightly over each braid. Sprinkle each loaf evenly with 1 tablespoon rolled oats.

7. Bake loaves in a 350°F oven until they are well browned and sound hollow when they are tapped lightly (45 to 50 minutes). Remove to wire racks to cool.

Makes 2 loaves.

Spicy Apple Upside-Down Cake

¼ cup butter or margarine

1½ cups firmly packed light brown sugar

2 small tart cooking apples, peeled, cored, and thinly sliced

1¾ cups all-purpose flour

2½ teaspoons baking powder

1 teaspoon ground cinnamon

¼ teaspoon *each* salt and ground nutmeg

⅛ teaspoon ground cloves

½ cup (¼ lb) butter or margarine, softened

1 egg

1 teaspoon vanilla

1 cup milk

Whipped cream (optional)

1. Melt the ¼ cup butter in a 9-inch-square or 10-inch-diameter baking pan over low heat. Add ½ cup of the brown sugar and cook, stirring constantly, until mixture bubbles all over (5 to 10 minutes). Remove from heat and arrange apple slices evenly in sugar mixture; set aside.

2. In a medium bowl, blend flour, baking powder, cinnamon, salt, nutmeg, and cloves.

3. Beat the ½ cup butter with remaining 1 cup brown sugar until light and fluffy. Beat in egg, then vanilla. Add flour mixture to butter mixture alternately with milk, mixing until smooth after each addition. Spread evenly over apples in prepared pan.

4. Bake in a 350°F oven until cake is well browned and tests done when a wooden pick is inserted near center (50 to 55 minutes).

5. While still warm, loosen edges with a spatula and turn cake out onto a serving plate. Cut in squares or wedges. Serve warm, with whipped cream if you wish.

Makes 6 to 8 servings.

Leek and Potato Soup

Leeks are one of the aristocrats of the onion family, with a flavor that is earthy yet suave. Joined with potatoes, they lend these qualities to a classic French soup.

6 medium leeks (2½ to 3 lbs)

¼ cup butter or margarine

⅛ teaspoon white pepper

¼ cup chopped fresh parsley

2 medium-size smooth-skinned potatoes (about 1 lb), peeled and diced

3½ cups Rich Chicken Broth (see page 9) *or* 2 cans (14½ oz *each*) chicken broth

½ cup half-and-half (light cream)

Salt (optional)

1. Cut off root ends of leeks; remove and discard coarse outer leaves. Cut off and discard green tops so that leeks are about 9 inches long. Split lengthwise, from leafy end, cutting to within about 1 inch of root end. Soak in cold water for several minutes; then separate leaves under running water to rinse away any clinging grit; drain. Slice about ¼ inch thick.

2. Melt butter in a 3-quart saucepan over medium heat; add leeks and cook, stirring often, until soft but not browned. Mix in pepper, parsley, potatoes, and broth. Bring to boiling, cover, reduce heat slightly, and boil gently until potatoes are very tender (25 to 30 minutes).

3. Purée mixture, about half at a time, in a blender or food processor until smooth. Return to cooking pan and stir in half-and-half. Taste, and add salt if needed. Reheat slowly to serving temperature, stirring often. (Do not boil.) Serve hot.

Makes 6 servings (about 7 cups).

Bernese Potato Soup

From Switzerland's capital city comes this velvety potato soup with cheese, good as a starter or as a meal in itself with a crusty loaf and a green salad.

¼ cup butter or margarine

1 medium onion, chopped

1 small carrot, chopped

1 stalk celery, with leaves, chopped

1 clove garlic, minced or pressed

A broiled topping of whipped cream completes savory Bongo Bongo Soup with a flourish.

¼ teaspoon *each* white pepper and dried marjoram

Pinch ground nutmeg

4 medium-size smooth-skinned potatoes (about 1½ lbs), peeled and diced

3½ cups Rich Chicken Broth (see page 9) *or* 2 cans (14½ oz *each*) chicken broth

1 cup milk

1 cup (¼ lb) shredded Swiss cheese

Salt (optional)

1. Melt butter in a 3- to 4-quart saucepan over medium heat. Add onion, carrot, celery, and garlic and cook, stirring often, until soft but not browned. Mix in pepper, marjoram, nutmeg, potatoes, and broth. Bring to boiling, cover, reduce heat slightly, and boil gently until potatoes are very tender (25 to 30 minutes).

2. Purée soup, about half at a time, in a blender or food processor until smooth. Return to cooking pan.

3. Gradually blend in milk and reheat until steaming hot. (Do not boil.) Stir in cheese, about ¼ cup at a time, until it is smoothly melted into soup. Taste, and add salt if needed. Serve at once.

Makes 6 to 8 servings (about 8 cups).

Bongo Bongo Soup

Inspired by a soup served at Trader Vic's many restaurants, Bongo Bongo is a smooth purée of fresh oysters and spinach. For the finishing touch, spoon whipped cream onto each serving (use heatproof bowls) and broil until the cream is tinged with golden brown. This final step is a handsome way of presenting cream soups.

1 bunch spinach (about ¾ lb)

3 tablespoons butter or margarine

1 small clove garlic, minced or pressed

2 cups milk

1 jar (10 fl oz) fresh oysters

1 cup whipping cream

1 teaspoon Worcestershire sauce

¾ teaspoon salt

⅛ teaspoon white pepper

1. Remove and discard stems from well-washed spinach. (You should have about 2 quarts leaves.) Place spinach in a large saucepan and stir, uncovered, over medium heat with no added liquid until spinach is limp (3 to 5 minutes). Drain well, pressing out excess moisture. Chop spinach coarsely and set it aside.

2. In a 2- to 3-quart saucepan, melt butter over medium heat. Add garlic and cook, stirring, until golden. (Do not brown.) Add milk and heat until it steams. Add oysters (with any liquid) and poach until edges ruffle (2 to 3 minutes). Remove pan from heat.

3. Transfer oyster mixture to a blender or food processor and add cooked spinach. Whirl or process until very smooth.

4. Return spinach and oyster mixture to cooking pan with ⅔ cup of the cream, Worcestershire sauce, salt, and pepper. Stir occasionally over medium heat until blended and steaming hot. (Do not boil.)

5. Whip remaining ⅓ cup cream until not quite stiff. Divide soup among heatproof bowls. Spoon whipped cream onto soup. Broil about 4 inches from heat until golden brown (2 to 3 minutes). Serve immediately.

Makes 4 servings (about 5 cups).

Peruvian Creole Soup

Pork is more a flavoring than a main ingredient of *sopa de criolla,* a favorite opening for a light meal of grilled chicken or fish.

- **1 loin pork chop, about ¾ inch thick (about ½ lb)**
- **1 to 2 teaspoons salad oil**
- **1 medium onion, finely chopped**
- **1 medium tomato, peeled, seeded, and chopped**
- **1 small dried hot red chile, finely crushed**
- **1 small clove garlic, minced or pressed**
- **½ teaspoon *each* salt and ground cumin**
- **¼ teaspoon ground turmeric**
- **3½ cups Rich Chicken Broth (see page 9) *or* 2 cans (14½ oz *each*) chicken broth**
- **2 egg yolks**
- **1 cup half-and-half (light cream)**
- **Chopped fresh parsley, for garnish**

1. Trim fat from pork chop, cut fat into small pieces, and reserve it. Trim meat and cut it into thin bite-size strips. Discard bone.

2. In a 3-quart saucepan, heat pork fat over medium heat until it coats pan; add a little salad oil if needed.

Discard solid pieces of fat. Add pork strips and onions and cook, stirring, until lightly browned. Mix in tomato, chile, garlic, salt, cumin, and turmeric.

3. Add broth, bring to boiling, cover, reduce heat, and simmer until pork is very tender (about 30 minutes). Meanwhile, in a small bowl, beat egg yolks with half-and-half.

4. After 30 minutes, gradually whisk about 1 cup of the hot broth into egg mixture; stir it vigorously into soup and continue stirring over medium-low heat until soup is steaming hot and slightly thickened. (Do not boil.) Taste, and add salt if needed.

5. Serve sprinkled with parsley.

Makes 4 servings (about 5½ cups).

French Alpine Soup

A veritable garden of vegetables—cauliflower, Swiss chard, carrot, celery, and onion—blends smoothly in this creamy, light green soup.

- **3 tablespoons butter or margarine**
- **1 medium onion, chopped**
- **1 stalk celery, chopped**
- **¼ cup thinly sliced carrot**
- **3 cups cauliflowerets**
- **2 cups lightly packed, coarsely chopped Swiss chard leaves (discard coarse stems)**
- **⅛ teaspoon white pepper**
- **¼ teaspoon dried marjoram**
- **Pinch cayenne pepper**
- **3½ cups Rich Chicken Broth (see page 9) *or* 2 cans (14½ oz *each*) chicken broth**
- **1 cup half-and-half (light cream)**
- **Salt (optional)**

1. Melt butter in a 3-quart saucepan over medium heat. Add onion, celery, and carrot; cook, stirring occasionally, until soft but not browned. Mix in cauliflower, chard, pepper, marjoram, cayenne, and broth.

2. Bring to boiling, reduce heat, cover, and simmer until cauliflower is very tender (10 to 12 minutes).

3. Whirl mixture in blender or food processor, about half at a time, until smooth.

4. Return to cooking pan, add half-and-half, and reheat to serving temperature. (Do not boil.) Taste, and add salt if needed. Serve hot.

Makes 6 servings (about 7 cups).

Dungeness Crab Bisque

When crab is in season, celebrate with this lusciously creamy soup as a first course, followed by a favorite chicken breast entrée.

- **1 medium Dungeness crab (about 2 lbs), cooked, cleaned, and cracked**
- **1 quart Fish Broth or Rich Chicken Broth (see page 9) *or* canned chicken broth**
- **2 sprigs parsley**
- **2 medium onions, thinly sliced**
- **1 cup dry white wine**
- **¼ cup butter or margarine**
- **¼ teaspoon dried tarragon**
- **¼ cup all-purpose flour**
- **⅛ teaspoon white pepper**
- **Pinch ground nutmeg**
- **1 cup half-and-half (light cream)**
- **½ cup whipping cream**
- **Salt (optional)**
- **3 tablespoons brandy**

1. Remove crab from shell, reserving shell. (You should have about 2½ cups crab.)

2. In a 3-quart saucepan, combine crab shell, broth, parsley, one of the sliced onions, and wine. Bring to boiling over medium heat, cover, reduce heat, and simmer for 30 minutes. Strain through a fine sieve or several thicknesses of dampened cheesecloth to remove all solids.

3. In same 3-quart pan, melt butter over medium heat. Add tarragon and remaining sliced onion. Cook, stirring often, until onion is soft but not browned. Stir in crab and cook for about 2 minutes more. Remove and reserve about ½ cup of the larger pieces of crab.

4. To remaining crab mixture in pan, add flour, pepper, and nutmeg; stir until bubbling. Gradually blend in strained broth. Bring to boiling, cover, reduce heat, and simmer for 15 minutes. Transfer mixture, about half at a time, to a blender or food processor. Whirl or process until smoothly puréed. Return to cooking pan.

5. Stir in half-and-half. Cook, stirring often, until steaming hot. (Do not boil.) Then add cream and reserved crab. Taste, and add salt if needed. Reheat to serving temperature. Just before serving, mix in brandy.

Makes 6 servings (about 6½ cups).

THE LIGHT TOUCH IN SOUPS

A Danish-Style Dinner

Danish Asparagus and Chicken Soup

Broiled Salmon with Orange-Mint Butter

Whole Green Beans   New Potatoes

Copenhagen-Style Ginger Sundaes

Pretzel-Shaped Butter Cookies

White Wine   Coffee

A velvety, pale green soup sets the festive mood for a candlelit dinner for four. A citrus- and mint-flavored butter seasons the salmon steaks as they broil, and the recipe makes enough so that you can also lavish the butter on the beans and potatoes.

The tender little butter cookies are packaged or from a Scandinavian bakery. A dry California Fumé Blanc is a good wine to accompany both the soup and the salmon.

Danish Asparagus and Chicken Soup

Chicken Breast and Broth (recipe follows)

¾ **pound asparagus**

1 **medium onion, finely chopped**

3 **tablespoons butter or margarine**

1½ **tablespoons all-purpose flour**

⅛ **teaspoon dried tarragon**

Pinch *each* ground nutmeg and white pepper

1 **cup half-and-half (light cream)**

1 **egg, slightly beaten**

2 **teaspoons lemon juice**

Salt (optional)

This inviting Danish menu in three courses is perfect for spring, when both asparagus—puréed in the creamy first-course soup—and salmon are in season. An enticing butter (made with orange and lemon peels and fresh mint) flavors salmon, green beans, and potatoes.

1. Prepare Chicken Breast and Broth according to directions; set meat and broth aside separately.

2. Break off and discard tough ends of asparagus. Cut off tips; cook, uncovered, in boiling salted water just until tender-crisp (2 to 3 minutes); drain and set aside. Slice remaining asparagus stems about ½ inch thick.

3. In a 3-quart saucepan, cook onion in butter over medium heat until soft but not browned. Mix in flour; cook until bubbly. Add tarragon, nutmeg, and pepper. Remove from heat and gradually blend in reserved chicken broth. Cook, stirring, until soup boils gently. Add asparagus stems.

4. Reduce heat, cover, and simmer until asparagus is tender (10 to 12 minutes). Transfer mixture to blender or food processor and whirl or process until smooth. Return asparagus purée to cooking pan.

5. Stir in half-and-half and reserved chicken breast. Cook, stirring, over medium heat until soup is steaming hot. Beat egg with lemon juice in a small bowl. Stir in a little of the hot soup. Blend egg mixture into hot soup. Cook, stirring, until hot but not boiling. Taste, and add salt if needed. Stir in reserved asparagus tips. Serve soup steaming hot.

Makes 4 servings (about 5 cups).

Chicken Breast and Broth In a 2- to 3-quart saucepan, combine 1 chicken breast (about 1 lb), cut into 2 pieces; 1 stalk celery (thinly sliced); 1 small onion (chopped); 1 teaspoon salt; 2 whole allspice; and 3 cups water. Bring to boiling, cover, reduce heat, and simmer for 45 minutes. Strain, reserving broth. Discard seasonings, bones, and skin. Cut chicken into thin bite-size pieces.

Broiled Salmon with Orange-Mint Butter

½ cup (¼ lb) butter or margarine, softened

½ teaspoon *each* grated orange and lemon peel

1 tablespoon *each* orange and lemon juice

¼ cup finely chopped fresh mint leaves *or* 1 tablespoon dried mint

⅛ teaspoon white pepper

4 salmon steaks, ¾ to 1 inch thick

Salad oil

1. In a medium bowl, beat butter until fluffy. Add orange and lemon peels; then gradually beat in orange and lemon juices until well combined. Blend in mint and pepper. Cover and refrigerate butter mixture to blend flavors (2 to 3 hours or overnight).

2. Remove butter from refrigerator to soften slightly while preparing salmon. Brush salmon steaks lightly with oil on both sides. Brush broiler rack lightly with oil. Arrange salmon steaks, slightly apart, on rack.

3. Broil, about 4 inches from heat, for 4 minutes. Turn salmon and dot each steak with a generous teaspoon of the orange-mint butter. Broil until salmon browns lightly and flakes easily when tested with a fork (4 to 5 minutes).

4. Serve salmon with additional orange-mint butter for each serving.

Makes 4 servings.

Copenhagen-Style Ginger Sundaes

¼ cup preserved ginger in syrup

2 tablespoons syrup from preserved ginger

⅓ cup white crème de cacao

8 generous scoops rich vanilla ice cream

Sweetened whipped cream

Chocolate curls, for garnish

1. Cut ginger in thin strips about 1 inch long. Place ginger strips, ginger syrup, and crème de cacao in a small bowl. Stir gently to thoroughly combine all ingredients. Cover and let stand at room temperature to blend flavors (1 to 4 hours).

2. To serve, place 2 scoops of ice cream in each of 4 chilled dessert dishes. Spoon ginger sauce evenly over the ice cream. Dollop whipped cream (or pipe it from a pastry bag, using a star tip) around the ice cream.

3. Garnish with chocolate curls and serve at once.

Makes 4 servings.

Two-Way Soups: Serve Hot or Cold

Some soups are as delicious cold as they are hot. That means you can enjoy them regardless of the weather outdoors—steaming soup when it's gray and blustery, chilled soup to refresh you on a muggy day.

Curried Pea Soup

When fresh peas are in season, it's worth the effort of shelling them for this piquantly seasoned soup. Otherwise, use about 2½ cups of frozen peas. When the soup is served hot, the curry flavor is assertive; chilled, it will taste more lemony. A dollop of yogurt is a nice finishing touch if you are serving the soup cold.

- **2 pounds fresh peas in shells**
- **¼ cup butter or margarine**
- **2 tablespoons salad oil**
- **2 medium onions, finely chopped**
- **1 large clove garlic, minced or pressed**
- **2 tablespoons curry powder**
- **1 teaspoon ground turmeric**
- **2 tablespoons all-purpose flour**
- **1 small head butter or Boston lettuce, shredded (about 4 cups, lightly packed)**
- **Grated peel and juice of 1 lemon**
- **2 teaspoons sugar**
- **1 quart Rich Chicken Broth (see page 9) or canned chicken broth**
- **1 cup half-and-half (light cream)**
- **Salt (optional)**

1. Shell peas. (You should have about 2½ cups.) Reserve about 2 tablespoons small peas to use as garnish.

2. In a 3½- to 4-quart saucepan, melt butter with oil over medium heat. Add onion and garlic and cook, stirring often, until soft but not browned. Blend in curry powder and turmeric, then flour. Add shredded lettuce, lemon peel and juice, sugar, and peas, except for the reserved 2 tablespoons. Remove from heat and gradually blend in broth.

3. Bring to boiling, stirring, over medium heat; then cover, reduce heat, and simmer until peas are just tender (8 to 10 minutes). Blend in half-and-half. Taste, and add salt if needed.

4. Transfer mixture, about a third at a time, to food processor or blender and process or whirl until smooth.

5. To serve cold, cover and refrigerate until thoroughly chilled. *Or* return to cooking pan and heat, stirring often, until steaming hot. Serve garnished with reserved uncooked peas.

Makes 6 to 8 servings (about 9 cups).

Peas cook with tender lettuce and piquant seasonings to make a creamy soup that is good hot or cold. Lemon zest is a pretty garnish.

Mussel Soup Billy-Bi

Once seen mostly in restaurants, fresh mussels now are often available from good fish markets. When you come upon them, it's an occasion to present them in this pale golden soup. Some trace the origin of this recipe to a restaurant in Deauville (in the Normandy region of France), where it is believed to have been created and named for a special customer.

- **2 quarts (about 3 lbs) uncooked mussels in shells**
- **2 tablespoons butter or margarine**
- **¼ teaspoon paprika**
- **4 shallots, finely chopped**
- **3 sprigs parsley**
- **¼ teaspoon whole white peppercorns**
- **1 cup dry white wine**
- **1½ to 2 cups Fish Broth or Rich Chicken Broth (see page 9) or 1 can (14½ oz) chicken broth**
- **2 cups whipping cream**
- **Salt (optional)**
- **Italian (flat-leaf) parsley, for garnish**

1. Discard any mussels that may have opened. Clean mussels by scraping off any barnacles. Then scrub with a stiff brush under running water to remove sand; drain.

2. Melt butter in a 4- to 5-quart kettle over medium heat. Add paprika and shallots; cook, stirring, until soft but not browned. Add mussels in shells, parsley, peppercorns, and wine. Bring to boiling, cover, reduce heat, and simmer until mussels have opened (6 to 8 minutes). Discard any mussels that remain closed.

3. Remove mussels from liquid. Strain cooking liquid through a dampened cloth and measure it. Add Fish Broth to make 1 quart. Return liquid to cooking pan (rinse pan after cooking to remove any sand).

4. Remove mussels from shells, discarding shells. (You should have about 2 cups.) Pinch out and discard the "beard" from any mussel that has one.

5. To liquid add cream. Bring to boiling over high heat. Reduce heat slightly and boil until soup is reduced by about a fourth. Lower heat to medium. Taste, and add salt if needed. Add mussels and cook just until heated through.

6. Serve hot. *Or* cool slightly; then cover and refrigerate until thoroughly chilled (several hours or overnight); stir well before serving. Garnish each serving with a leaf or two of parsley.

Makes 4 to 6 servings (6 to 7 cups).

Sherried Artichoke Soup

When you offer this soup cold, at the very last moment pour about a tablespoon of whipping cream into the center of each serving (without stirring) to accent the subtle artichoke flavor.

- **2 tablespoons butter or margarine**
- **1 medium onion, finely chopped**
- **1 small clove garlic, minced or pressed**
- **2 tablespoons all-purpose flour**
- **Pinch ground nutmeg**
- **1¾ cups Rich Chicken Broth (see page 9) or 1 can (14½ oz) chicken broth**
- **1 package (9 oz) frozen artichoke hearts, thawed**
- **2 tablespoons chopped fresh parsley**
- **1 cup half-and-half (light cream)**
- **Salt and white pepper**
- **3 tablespoons dry sherry**
- **Snipped fresh chives**

1. In a 2- to 3-quart saucepan, melt butter over medium heat; add onion and cook until soft. Stir in garlic, then flour and nutmeg. Cook, stirring, until mixture is bubbly. Remove from heat and gradually blend in broth.

2. Add artichokes and parsley to broth mixture. Cook over medium heat, stirring occasionally, until artichokes are tender (6 to 8 minutes). Remove 3 or 4 of the artichoke hearts; chop and reserve them.

3. Purée the remaining artichoke mixture in a blender or food processor until smooth. Return purée to cooking pan; blend in half-and-half and reserved chopped artichokes. Season to taste with salt and pepper.

4. Cook over medium heat, stirring often, until steaming hot. Mix in sherry. Serve hot. *Or* cool slightly; then cover and refrigerate and serve cold. Sprinkle chives over each serving.

Makes 4 servings (about 6 cups).

Cream of Fresh Tomato Soup

Juicily ripe fresh tomatoes make all the difference in the flavor of this orange-spiked cream soup. It seems that such tomatoes ripen during the hottest weeks of the year—all the more reason to serve this soup cold.

- **2 pounds (about 4 large) tomatoes, peeled and chopped**
- **2 large onions, chopped**
- **2 large carrots, sliced**
- **2 tablespoons sugar**
- **Half a bay leaf**
- **¾ teaspoon salt**
- **⅛ teaspoon white pepper**
- **A 3-inch strip lemon peel**
- **1 quart Rich Chicken Broth (see page 9) or canned chicken broth**
- **2 tablespoons *each* butter or margarine, softened, and all-purpose flour**
- **1⅓ cups half-and-half (light cream)**
- **Thinly shredded peel of 2 oranges, for garnish**

1. In a 4- to 5-quart kettle, combine tomatoes, onions, carrots, sugar, bay leaf, salt, pepper, lemon peel, and chicken broth. Bring to boiling over moderately high heat, cover, reduce heat, and simmer for 30 minutes. Remove and discard bay leaf and lemon peel.

2. In a small bowl, mix butter and flour until smooth; set aside.

3. Transfer tomato mixture, a third to a fourth at a time, to a food processor or blender and process or whirl until smooth. Return to pan over medium heat. Stir in butter mixture, about a fourth at a time, mixing until soup thickens and boils.

4. Remove soup from heat and add half-and-half, all at once, stirring to blend. Return soup to heat and cook, stirring occasionally, until steaming hot. (Do not boil.) Taste, and add salt if needed. For a cold soup, remove from heat after thickening, blend in half-and-half, and refrigerate until chilled.

5. Serve sprinkled with orange peel.

Makes 6 to 8 servings (8 to 10 cups).

Chilled Soups for Hot Weather

When the temperature soars and it's as hot outdoors as in, most people prefer to cool off with cold food and drink. That is no reason not to enjoy soup with dinner or as the main dish of a lunch or supper.

Here are some cold soups for just such times. Two need no cooking at all, and the others can be made quickly in the cool of the morning and then stored in the refrigerator until you are ready for them.

Frosty Watercress Soup

For a finishing touch, into each serving of soup pour a little cream, grind a dash of pepper, and add a sprig of watercress. This cold soup makes an appealing summer lunch with plump croissant sandwiches.

- **2 bunches watercress (about 12 oz)**
- **2 tablespoons butter or margarine**
- **1 medium onion, chopped**
- **1 shallot, chopped**
- **1 bunch (about 6) green onions, sliced (use part of tops)**
- **2 tablespoons all-purpose flour**
- **¼ teaspoon salt**
- **⅛ teaspoon white pepper**
- **3½ cups Rich Chicken Broth (see page 9) or 2 cans (14½ oz each) chicken broth**
- **1 cup peas (fresh or frozen)**
- **1 cup whipping cream**
- **Additional whipping cream and freshly ground white pepper, for garnish**

1. Rinse watercress and drain well. Remove and discard coarse stems. (You should have about 6 cups watercress leaves and tender sprigs, lightly packed.)

2. In a 3-quart saucepan, melt butter over medium heat. Add onion, shallot, and green onions. Cook, stirring occasionally, until soft but not browned. Blend in flour, salt, and pepper, stirring until bubbly. Remove from heat and gradually blend in chicken broth. Bring to boiling, cover, reduce heat, and simmer for 15 minutes. Mix in peas and simmer, cov-

ered, for 3 minutes. Then stir in watercress, reserving 12 sprigs for garnish. Cover, remove from heat, and let stand for 5 minutes.

3. Purée watercress mixture, about half at a time, in a blender or food processor until smooth. Transfer to a glass bowl. Blend in whipping cream. Taste, and add salt if needed.

4. Cover and refrigerate until thoroughly chilled (3 to 5 hours or overnight). Serve cold, garnishing each serving by pouring about 2 tablespoons whipping cream into center and topping with a reserved watercress sprig or two and a grind of pepper.

Makes 6 servings (about 6½ cups).

Guadalajara Avocado Soup

This cold soup is of Mexican origin. A splash of tequila adds an edge of excitement to the smooth, delicious avocado cream. To preserve its fresh green color, prepare the soup no more than three hours before serving.

- **3 large soft-ripe avocados**
- **4 green onions, thinly sliced (use part of tops)**
- **1¾ cups Rich Chicken Broth (see page 9) or 1 can (14½ oz) chicken broth**
- **2 tablespoons lime or lemon juice**
- **½ teaspoon *each* salt and ground cumin**
- **Pinch cayenne pepper**
- **2 tablespoons tequila**
- **2 cups half-and-half (light cream)**
- **Thin lime slices, for garnish**

1. Peel and pit avocados; dice coarsely. (You should have about 4 cups.) Place in blender or food processor with green onions, broth, lime juice, salt, cumin, and cayenne. Whirl or process until very smooth.

2. Pour into a large glass bowl and blend in tequila, then half-and-half. Cover and refrigerate until thoroughly chilled (2 to 3 hours).

3. Before serving, stir well to blend. Serve soup cold, garnishing each serving with a lime slice.

Makes 6 servings (about 5½ cups).

Vichyssoise

The French name leads some to think that this classic cold soup originated in France, but in truth it was probably created in the kitchen of a New York hotel. This recipe yields a generous eight to ten servings and is perfect for warm weather entertaining.

- **5 medium leeks (2 to 2½ lbs)**
- **2 tablespoons butter or margarine**
- **1 small onion, finely chopped**
- **3 medium-size smooth-skinned potatoes (1 to 1¼ lbs), peeled and diced**
- **2 teaspoons salt**
- **⅛ teaspoon white pepper**
- **1 quart boiling water**
- **1 cup milk**
- **2 cups half-and-half (light cream)**
- **1 cup cold whipping cream**
- **Snipped fresh chives, for garnish**

1. Cut off root ends of leeks; remove and discard coarse outer leaves. Cut off and discard green tops so that leeks are about 8 inches long. Split lengthwise, from leafy end, cutting to within about 1 inch of root end. Soak in cold water for several minutes; then separate leaves under running water to rinse away any clinging grit; drain. Slice about ¼ inch thick.

2. Melt butter in a 3- to 4-quart saucepan over medium heat; add leeks and onion, and cook, stirring often, until soft but not browned. Mix in potatoes, salt, pepper, and boiling water. Bring mixture to boiling, cover, reduce heat slightly, and boil gently until potatoes are very tender (25 to 30 minutes).

3. Purée mixture, about half at a time, in a blender or food processor until smooth. Return to cooking pan. Blend in milk and half-and-half. Stir over medium heat until steaming hot. Strain into a large bowl to remove any lumps. Cover and refrigerate until thoroughly chilled (3 to 5 hours or overnight).

4. Using a whisk, blend in cream. Taste, and add salt if needed. (After adding cream, soup can be refrigerated again for up to 6 hours before serving. Stir well to blend before serving.)

5. Serve sprinkled with chives.

Makes 8 to 10 servings (9 to 10 cups).

Feathery fronds of fresh dill or snippets of chives accent a classic cold soup, Creamy Pink Borsch. Serve it with thinly sliced black bread and butter as a first course.

Creamy Pink Borsch

With black bread and butter, this fresh beet soup is a handsome beginning for a warm weather meal.

- **3 medium-size beets (1½ to 2 lbs with tops)**
- **Salted water**
- **2 tablespoons butter or margarine**
- **1 small onion, chopped**
- **2 teaspoons brown sugar**
- **¼ teaspoon salt**
- **Pinch *each* ground cloves and white pepper**
- **3 cups Rich Chicken Broth (see page 9) *or* canned chicken broth**
- **1 cup sour cream**
- **1 tablespoon lemon juice**
- **Additional sour cream and snipped fresh chives or dill, for garnish**

1. Cut off all but about 1 inch of beet tops. (Reserve greens to cook separately as a vegetable if you wish.) Scrub beets well. Place in a large pan with salted water to cover. Bring to boiling over high heat, cover, reduce heat, and boil gently until beets are tender (30 to 35 minutes). Drain and let stand until beets are cool enough to handle. Peel and dice cooked beets. (You should have about 2 cups.)

2. In a 2½- to 3-quart saucepan, melt butter over medium heat. Add onion and cook until soft but not browned. Mix in brown sugar, salt, cloves, pepper, and diced beets. Add broth, bring to boiling, cover, reduce heat, and simmer for 20 minutes.

3. Purée mixture, about half at a time, in blender or food processor until smooth. To second portion add sour cream and whirl until well blended. Combine both portions in a glass bowl. Blend in lemon juice. Taste, and add salt if needed. Cover and refrigerate for 3 to 5 hours or overnight.

4. Top with sour cream and chives.

Makes 6 servings (about 6 cups).

Gazpacho, Uxmal Style

With two warm countries—Spain and Mexico—as its source, it is no wonder that gazpacho is a soup that is always served cold. This version is about as crisp as any soup can be, because it contains so many chopped fresh vegetables.

- **1 large can (28 oz) whole tomatoes**
- **1 tablespoon red wine vinegar**
- **3 tablespoons olive oil**
- **1 cup tomato juice**
- **1 clove garlic, minced or pressed**
- **1 teaspoon salt**
- **½ teaspoon *each* sugar and dried oregano**
- **1 stalk celery, finely chopped**
- **1 small hot fresh green chile, seeded and finely chopped *or* ⅛ teaspoon cayenne pepper**
- **½ cup peeled, seeded, and chopped cucumber**
- **¼ cup *each* finely chopped mild red onion and seeded green bell pepper**
- **¼ cup sliced pimiento-stuffed green olives**
- **1 avocado, peeled, seeded, and diced**
- **Lime wedges, Garlic Croutons (see page 7), sour cream, crumbled crisp bacon, and cilantro (Chinese parsley) sprigs, as condiments**

1. Reserving 2 whole tomatoes, place remaining tomatoes and their liquid in blender or food processor with vinegar, olive oil, tomato juice, garlic, salt, sugar, and oregano. Whirl or process until smooth.

2. Pour puréed tomato mixture into a large bowl. To it add reserved tomatoes, finely chopped. Then mix in celery, green chile, cucumber, onion, bell pepper, and olives. Cover and refrigerate for at least 8 hours or overnight (up to 3 days).

3. Just before serving, mix in avocado. Serve cold, passing small bowls of condiments to add at table to taste.

Makes 6 to 8 servings (about 7 cups).

From Fruit Basket to Soup Bowl

It's said that a resourceful cook can make a good soup from anything. If you have never tried a fruit soup, consider serving one as a breakfast main dish—or for dessert.

Fruit soups are something like a sparkly, lightly cooked fruit compote. You have the option of serving them hot or cold.

These fruit soup recipes follow the seasons: Rhubarb Soup with White Wine for spring, Blueberry-Orange Soup and Raspberry-Peach Soup for summer and early autumn, and Winter Fruit Soup with mixed dried fruits for the months in between.

Rhubarb Soup with White Wine

- 4 cups diced rhubarb (1 to 1¼ lbs)
- 1 cup water
- ¾ cup sugar
- A 2-inch cinnamon stick
- 1 tablespoon cornstarch, mixed with 1 tablespoon water
- ½ cup dry white wine
- Few drops red food coloring (optional)
- Toasted sliced almonds, for garnish

1. In a 3-quart pan, combine rhubarb, water, sugar, and cinnamon stick. Bring to boiling over high heat; then reduce heat and simmer, uncovered, for 15 minutes.

2. Blend in cornstarch mixture and bring to boiling again over high heat, stirring until soup is thickened and clear.

3. Remove from heat and blend in wine. If you prefer a pinker color, blend in a drop or two of food coloring.

4. Serve warm. *Or* cool slightly; then cover and refrigerate until thoroughly chilled (2 to 3 hours or overnight). Sprinkle a few almonds over each serving.

Makes 4 to 6 servings (about 3 cups).

Raspberry-Peach Soup

- ¾ cup *each* water and sugar
- 1 large peach, peeled and thinly sliced
- 2 baskets (about 1½ cups *each*) raspberries
- 1 tablespoon cornstarch, mixed with 2 tablespoons water
- 2 teaspoons lemon juice
- 1 tablespoon framboise or kirsch (clear fruit brandy)
- Whipped cream

1. In a 2- to 3-quart saucepan, combine water and sugar. Bring to boiling over high heat, stirring until sugar dissolves. Add peach and boil gently for 2 minutes. Add raspberries and bring again to boiling; boil for 1 minute.

2. Blend in cornstarch mixture; bring again to boiling, stirring until thickened and clear.

3. Remove from heat and stir in lemon juice and framboise. Serve hot. *Or* cool slightly; then cover and refrigerate until cold (2 to 3 hours or overnight). Spoon a dollop of whipped cream over each serving.

Makes 4 to 6 servings (about 3½ cups).

Blueberry-Orange Soup

- 1 orange
- ⅔ cup *each* water and sugar
- 3 cups blueberries
- ⅛ teaspoon grated nutmeg
- 1 tablespoon cornstarch, mixed with 2 tablespoons water
- 2 teaspoons lemon juice
- Whipping cream

1. Grate 2 teaspoons orange peel and reserve it. Squeeze juice from orange; strain out seeds if necessary.

2. In a 2- to 3-quart saucepan, combine orange juice, water, and sugar. Bring to boiling over high heat, stirring until sugar dissolves. Add blueberries and bring again to boiling; boil for 1 minute. Blend in reserved orange peel and nutmeg; then add cornstarch mixture. Bring to boiling again, stirring until soup is thickened and clear.

3. Remove from heat and stir in lemon juice. Serve hot. Or cool slightly; then cover and refrigerate until cold (2 to 3 hours or overnight). Accompany with cream to pour over soup, or whip cream until slightly thickened and spoon onto each serving.

Makes 4 servings (3 cups).

Winter Fruit Soup

- 2 packages (8 oz *each*) mixed dried fruits *or* about 3 cups mixed dried prunes, apricots, pears, peaches, and apples
- ½ cup sugar
- 2 tablespoons quick-cooking tapioca
- 3 cups water
- Grated peel and juice of 1 orange
- A 2- to 3-inch cinnamon stick
- Pinch salt
- Whipping cream

1. Cut larger fruits, such as pears and peaches, into ½-inch-wide strips.

2. In a 2- to 3-quart saucepan, combine fruits, sugar, tapioca, water, orange peel and juice, cinnamon stick, and salt. Bring to boiling over high heat, stirring mixture until sugar dissolves.

3. Cover, reduce heat, and simmer until fruits are plump and tender but still retain their shapes (about 20 to 25 minutes).

4. Serve hot or at room temperature. Accompany with whipping cream to pour into each serving to taste, or whipped cream to spoon onto each serving.

Makes 6 servings (about 5¾ cups).

All the colors of the rainbow and the flavors of four seasons can be found in this tempting assortment of fruit soups. Shown from top to bottom are Rhubarb Soup with White Wine, Winter Fruit Soup, Blueberry-Orange Soup, and Raspberry-Peach Soup. While most people will find them too sweet to serve for a first course, they are delightful for breakfast or for dessert.

THE LIGHT TOUCH IN SOUPS

SATISFYING FULL-MEAL SOUPS

turdy soups such as those in this chapter must surely be the model for every one-dish meal. Into one big kettle go savory vegetables; juicy meats, chicken, or fish; pungent onions, garlic, and herbs; and often rice, dried beans, or pasta. What emerges hours later is a melting pot of flavors—a full-meal soup. When you're really hungry, you couldn't ask for a more filling meal. All you need to add to make a complete repast are some good bread or crackers, a salad or crisp raw vegetables, and fruit or a simple, light dessert.

Although you might assume that hearty soups are hours in the making and impractical for time-pressed cooks, that isn't so. The first four recipes in this chapter are designed for short-order cooking; all can be made in about an hour or less, so you can serve them with little advance notice.

Other soups, although they may take more time to cook, can be started one day, refrigerated, and then finished the next. And just about all can be frozen and reheated (with the help of the tips on pages 6–7). Most soup enthusiasts agree that flavors improve, pease-porridge-in-a-pot fashion, when they are allowed to blend for a day or so.

To complement your fine, homemade soup, you might like to try your hand at baking crackers and other crispy flatbreads. You will find recipes to start you off on pages 54–55.

For those who occasionally crave the flavors and textures characteristic of Chinese soups, there is a collection of them on page 49. While they are not usually served as main dishes in China, they are so complete in all the elements Westerners expect that you can enjoy them as such.

Red-and-White Fish Chowder (the recipe is on page 53) is a quick and hearty soup of red snapper, potatoes, red peppers, and cream.

Short-Order Soups

When you start with ground meat or sausage, soup can be a speedy main dish for supper. You need not spend much time on other dishes because the entire meal is in one bowl.

Tastefully chosen seasonings and vegetables will give your quick-cooking soup plenty of flavor, especially if you start with a homemade stock (see pages 8–9) that you've tucked away in the freezer for just such an occasion.

These recipes all use meat; you will find other time-saving soups in the sections on soups made from poultry (page 44) and seafood (page 50).

Polish Sausage and Cabbage Soup

Here is a colorful soup made with a garlicky sausage that lends its flavor to all the delicious fresh vegetables around it. Serve the soup with milk or beer, dark bread with butter, and a warm fruit dessert such as an apple crisp.

- **2 tablespoons butter or margarine**
- **1 stalk celery, thinly sliced**
- **1 medium onion, slivered**
- **1 medium-size sweet red or green bell pepper, seeded and chopped**
- **1 medium potato (about ½ lb), diced**
- **1 pound Polish sausage, cut in 1-inch pieces**
- **1 bay leaf**
- **3½ cups Rich Chicken Broth (see page 9) or 2 cans (14½ oz each) chicken broth**
- **¼ cup chopped fresh parsley**
- **2 cups finely shredded cabbage**
- **Sour cream**

1. Melt butter in a 3- to 4-quart saucepan over medium heat. Add celery, onion, and bell pepper and cook, stirring occasionally, until onion is soft but not browned.

2. Add potato, Polish sausage, bay leaf, and broth. Bring to a gentle boil, cover, reduce heat, and simmer until potato is tender (about 20 minutes).

3. Remove and discard bay leaf. Remove about 1 cup of the vegetables with a little of the broth to a blender or food processor. Whirl or process until smooth; then return to soup mixture in pan.

4. Add parsley and cabbage to soup. Stir often over medium heat until soup is steaming hot and cabbage is wilted and bright green (3 to 5 minutes).

5. Serve with sour cream to spoon onto each serving to taste.

Makes 4 to 6 servings (about 8 cups).

Quick Meatball and Zucchini Soup

Here is a soup that is a bargain in both time *and* money: The recipe makes four to six servings from just 1 pound of ground beef. Complete the menu with crusty rolls and a jug red wine, plus ice cream and chocolate chip cookies for dessert.

- **Meatballs (recipe follows)**
- **1 tablespoon olive oil or salad oil**
- **1 large onion, slivered**
- **1 clove garlic, minced or pressed**
- **1 stalk celery, thinly sliced**
- **1 medium carrot, thinly sliced**
- **1 teaspoon dried basil**
- **¼ teaspoon *each* dried thyme and oregano**
- **1 large can (28 oz) tomatoes**
- **1¾ cups Sturdy Beef Broth (see page 8) or 1 can (14½ oz) regular-strength beef broth**
- **1 cup *each* dry red wine and water**
- **¼ cup orzo (rice-shaped pasta) or other tiny soup pasta**
- **3 medium zucchini (about 1 lb)**
- **Salt (optional)**
- **Grated Parmesan cheese**

1. In a 4- to 6-quart Dutch oven, brown meatballs carefully in heated oil over medium heat, removing them as they brown. To same pan, add onion, garlic, celery, and carrot. Cook for 5 minutes, stirring occasionally.

2. Sprinkle with basil, thyme, and oregano; then add tomatoes (coarsely chopped) and their liquid, broth, wine, and water. Return meatballs to pan. Bring soup to boiling, cover, reduce heat, and simmer for 30 minutes.

3. Add orzo and cook, covered, at a gentle boil until pasta is nearly tender (12 to 15 minutes). Meanwhile, scrub zucchini and cut off ends. Cut lengthwise into quarters; then slice thinly.

4. Add zucchini to soup and cook, uncovered, until zucchini is just tender (4 to 6 minutes). Taste, and add salt if needed.

5. Serve with Parmesan cheese to sprinkle over each serving to taste.

Makes 4 to 6 servings (about 13 cups).

Meatballs In a medium bowl, beat 1 egg; mix in ¼ cup *each* soft bread crumbs and grated Parmesan cheese, ¾ teaspoon salt, and 1 clove garlic (minced or pressed). Lightly mix in 1 pound lean ground beef. Shape into 1-inch meatballs.

Beefy Soup au Pistou

This traditional French soup is usually made without any meat, but ground beef makes it even better. The word *pistou* refers to the pesto-like paste of basil and garlic that flavors the soup. With it, serve a simple green salad, a baguette of French bread with sweet butter, and a light red wine. Then spoon sweetened fresh strawberries over vanilla ice cream for dessert.

- **1½ pounds ground lean beef, crumbled**
- **2 tablespoons olive oil**
- **1 large onion, thinly slivered**
- **1 clove garlic, minced or pressed**
- **1 large can (28 oz) tomatoes**
- **3½ cups Sturdy Beef Broth (see page 8) or 2 cans (14½ oz each) regular-strength beef broth**
- **2 cups water**
- **2 teaspoons salt**
- **¼ teaspoon pepper**
- **2 medium potatoes (about 1 lb), cut in ½-inch cubes**
- **1 pound green beans, cut in 1-inch pieces**
- **Boiling salted water**
- **¼ pound vermicelli, broken in half**
- **½ cup finely shredded Gruyère or Swiss cheese**
- **Pistou (recipe follows)**
- **Additional shredded Gruyère or Swiss cheese**

1. Cook ground beef in heated oil in a 5- to 6-quart kettle over medium heat, stirring often. As meat begins to brown, stir in onion and continue cooking until onion is soft. Stir in garlic. Add tomatoes (coarsely chopped) and their liquid, broth, water, salt, pepper, and potatoes.

Easy Lamb, Spinach, and Garbanzo Soup

Fresh lemon accents a savory soup with North African flavors. It is made with ground lamb and tastes good with warm pocket bread, beer, and tangerines or a citrus-flavored sherbet for dessert.

1 pound ground lean lamb, crumbled

1 tablespoon olive oil or salad oil

1 large onion, thinly slivered

1 stalk celery, finely chopped

2 cloves garlic, minced or pressed

½ teaspoon *each* salt and ground cumin

⅛ teaspoon ground allspice

1 can (15 oz) garbanzos (ceci beans or chick-peas)

1 can (15 oz) tomato purée

1¾ cups Rich Chicken Broth (see page 9) *or* 1 can (14½ oz) chicken broth

2 bunches (about 12 oz *each*) spinach

1 tablespoon grated lemon peel

Plain yogurt or sour cream

1. In a 3- to 4-quart saucepan over medium heat, cook lamb in heated oil, stirring often, until meat loses its pink color. Add onion and celery; cook, stirring often, until onion is soft. Mix in garlic, salt, cumin, and allspice.

2. Add garbanzos and their liquid, tomato purée, and broth. Bring to boiling, cover, reduce heat, and simmer for 30 minutes.

3. Meanwhile, wash spinach and drain well; discard stems. Slice leaves crosswise into about ½-inch-wide strips. (You should have about 2 quarts.) Set spinach aside.

4. After soup has simmered for 30 minutes, add spinach and cook, uncovered, stirring often, until soup returns to boiling. Mix in lemon peel. Taste, and add salt if needed.

5. Serve with yogurt or sour cream to top each serving.

Makes 4 to 6 servings (about 12 cups).

Beefy Soup au Pistou gets its name from a pungent paste of basil and garlic.

2. Bring to boiling, cover, reduce heat, and simmer for 1 hour. Meanwhile, cook green beans, uncovered, in a large quantity of boiling salted water until they are tender-crisp (6 to 8 minutes). Drain and rinse with cold water to stop cooking; drain and set aside.

3. After soup has cooked for 1 hour, add vermicelli and boil gently, uncovered, stirring occasionally, until it is just tender (10 to 12 minutes). Add green beans and cook until they are heated through.

4. Add the ½ cup Gruyère cheese, about a fourth at a time, stirring after each addition until cheese melts.

5. Place Pistou in a warm tureen, add soup, and stir until soup and Pistou are well blended. Serve at once with additional shredded cheese to add to each serving to taste.

Makes 6 to 8 servings (about 4 quarts).

Pistou In blender, combine ¼ cup olive oil, 3 cloves garlic (minced or pressed), ½ cup lightly packed fresh basil leaves (or 2 tablespoons dried basil and ½ cup lightly packed, chopped fresh parsley), ¼ teaspoon *each* salt and sugar, and 1 tablespoon red wine vinegar. Whirl until smooth. Makes about ⅓ cup.

Meaty Soups

At some time we have all had the comforting experience of coming in from the cold, wet outdoors to a cozy kitchen steamy with the aroma from a kettle of soup that had been simmering all day. It seemed the very essence of security and warmth. No one would call such soups timesavers, but they are well-remembered childhood favorites.

Here you will find those slowly cooked soups that begin with a hefty pot of meaty bones—beef, pork or ham, or lamb. Remember, you can make all these soups a day or more in advance. Reheat them just before serving, waiting until this final stage to add any bright green vegetables needing only brief cooking.

Sunday Night Vegetable-Beef Soup

While you are waiting for your portion of this traditional soup to cool a little, you might look for your name in the alphabet noodles. The soup goes well with nutty whole-grain crackers, milk, and favorite cheeses, then fresh fruit for dessert.

- **3 to 3½ pounds beef short ribs**
- **2 tablespoons butter or margarine**
- **2 medium onions, finely chopped**
- **2 stalks celery, thinly sliced**
- **3 cloves garlic, slivered**
- **1 sweet red or green bell pepper, seeded and chopped**
- **1 teaspoon chili powder**
- **1 large can (28 oz) tomatoes**
- **2 large carrots, thinly sliced**
- **2 medium-size red-skinned potatoes (about 1 lb), scrubbed (unpeeled) and diced**
- **1 bay leaf**
- **2 teaspoons salt**
- **¼ teaspoon pepper**
- **½ teaspoon dried marjoram**
- **2 quarts water**
- **½ cup alphabet noodles or other tiny soup pasta**
- **½ cup chopped fresh parsley**

1. In a 6- to 8-quart kettle or Dutch oven over medium heat, brown short ribs well on all sides in heated butter. As you turn short ribs to brown last side, add onions, celery, garlic, and bell pepper around them, stirring occasionally until vegetables are limp. Sprinkle with chili powder.

2. Add tomatoes (coarsely chopped) and their liquid, carrots, potatoes, bay leaf, salt, pepper, marjoram, and water. Bring to boiling, cover, reduce heat, and simmer until meat is very tender (3 to 4 hours).

3. Remove and discard bay leaf. Remove short ribs with a slotted spoon. When they are cool enough to handle, remove meat from bones and return it to soup in chunks; discard fat and bones. If possible, cover and refrigerate soup for several hours or overnight.

4. To serve, skim and discard surface fat from soup. Bring to boiling over medium-high heat. Add noodles and boil gently, uncovered, until noodles are tender (10 to 12 minutes). Taste soup, and add salt if needed. Stir in parsley and serve at once.

Makes 6 to 8 servings (about 4 quarts).

Petite Marmite

Here is another soup hearty with beef. This one is French in origin and has the distinction of being cooked in the oven. It takes its name from the deep earthenware casserole (*marmite*) in which it bakes.

If you wish to make the soup ahead of time, you can proceed through Step 4. After baking for about 4 hours, cool the casserole; then refrigerate it. To serve, let it stand at room temperature for about an hour. Then proceed with Step 5.

Either way, complement the soup's subtle spiciness by serving it with a velvety red wine.

- **3½ to 4 pounds beef shanks, sliced about 1 inch thick**
- **1 tablespoon *each* butter or margarine and salad oil**
- **1 pound chicken wings**
- **½ pound chicken livers**
- **2 medium onions, slivered**
- **2 cloves garlic, minced or pressed**
- **½ teaspoon dried thyme**
- **2 quarts hot water**
- **1 bay leaf**
- **3 sprigs parsley**
- **¼ teaspoons *each* whole cloves, whole allspice, and black peppercorns**
- **3 or 4 leeks**
- **2 small turnips (about ½ lb), peeled and cut in sixths**
- **1 stalk celery, thinly sliced**
- **3 medium carrots, thinly sliced**
- **1 teaspoon salt**
- **Toasted Cheese Croutons (recipe follows) or Herbed Sourdough Thins (see page 54)**

Try this beefy vegetable soup with alphabet noodles for a Sunday evening at home.

1. In a large, heavy frying pan over medium heat, brown beef shanks, three or four at a time, in heated mixture of butter and oil. As they brown, transfer shanks to a deep 5- to 6-quart marmite. Brown chicken wings and add them to marmite. Then brown chicken livers; remove to a shallow bowl, cover, and refrigerate until Step 5. In the same pan, cook onions, stirring often, until soft and lightly browned; mix in garlic and thyme. Add onion mixture to marmite. Add a little of the water to frying pan, stirring to loosen brown drippings; add mixture to marmite.

2. Cut a double thickness of cheesecloth 8 to 10 inches square. In center of cheesecloth, place bay leaf, parsley, cloves, allspice, and peppercorns. Tie corners of cloth in center to enclose seasonings securely; add to marmite.

3. Cut off root ends of leeks; then cut off green tops so that leeks are about 5 inches long. Remove coarse outer leaves. Rinse well to remove all grit between the leaves. Slice leeks about ¼ inch thick and add to marmite with turnips, celery, carrots, and salt. Add remaining hot water.

4. Cover marmite and place in a 350°F oven. Bake, stirring once or twice, until beef is tender and broth is richly flavored (3½ to 4 hours).

5. Add browned chicken livers, return to oven, and bake for about 45 minutes more.

6. With tongs, remove and discard seasonings in cheesecloth. Skim and discard surface fat if necessary. Taste broth, and add salt if needed.

7. Serve soup in hot individual bowls accompanied by warm Toasted Cheese Croutons either floating atop soup or to eat as crackers.

Makes 6 servings (about 15 cups).

Toasted Cheese Croutons Slice an 8-ounce baguette (long, thin loaf of French bread) crosswise to make 24 thin slices. In a small pan over medium heat, melt 2 tablespoons butter or margarine; add 1 tablespoon olive oil and 1 small clove garlic (minced or pressed). Place bread slices in a single layer on a baking sheet. Brush with the butter mixture. Bake in a 300°F oven until crisp and lightly browned (20 to 25 minutes). Sprinkle evenly with 1 cup thinly shredded Gruyère or Swiss cheese. Place about 4 inches below broiler and broil until cheese melts and browns lightly (2 to 3 minutes). Serve croutons hot. Makes 24.

Fresh spring vegetables, ham, and veal shanks combine in this hearty meal-in-a-bowl.

Springtime Veal and Vegetable Soup

The meaty veal shanks known in Italian cooking as *osso buco* add real substance to the stock that unites this enticing soup. With fresh green vegetables added just before you serve it, the soup needs few accompaniments beyond a good loaf of French bread, butter, and a full-bodied white wine.

6 leeks

2 medium onions, slivered

2 tablespoons butter or margarine

2 cloves garlic, minced or pressed

3 medium carrots, thinly sliced

4 medium-size, smooth-skinned potatoes (1½ to 2 lbs), sliced about ¼ inch thick

1 ham hock (½ to ¾ lb)

3 to 4 pounds veal shanks, cut in about 2-inch slices

½ teaspoon dried savory

¼ teaspoon white pepper

2 quarts water

½ pound asparagus

⅓ cup shelled fresh or frozen peas

Salt (optional)

¼ cup chopped fresh parsley

1. Cut off root ends of leeks; remove and discard coarse outer leaves. Cut off and discard green tops so that leeks are about 8 inches long. Split lengthwise, from leafy end, cutting to within about 1 inch of root end. Soak in cold water for several minutes; then separate leaves under running water to rinse away any clinging grit; drain. Slice about ¼ inch thick.

2. In a 6- to 8-quart kettle, cook leeks and onions in heated butter over medium heat, stirring often, until soft but not browned. Mix in garlic and carrots. Add potatoes, ham hock, veal shanks, savory, pepper, and water. Bring slowly to boiling, cover, reduce heat, and simmer until veal and ham are very tender (2½ to 3 hours).

3. Meanwhile, snap off and discard fibrous ends of asparagus. Slice stalks diagonally about ½ inch thick, keeping tips separate. Set aside.

4. Remove ham hock from soup; when it is cool enough to handle, remove and discard bones and skin. Return meat to soup in chunks. Increase heat to moderate. Stir in asparagus slices and cook, uncovered, for 5 minutes. Then mix in asparagus tips and peas; cook, uncovered, just until asparagus is tender-crisp (about 3 minutes). Taste soup, and add salt if needed. Stir in parsley.

5. To serve, place a veal shank in each bowl; then spoon vegetables and broth over and around it.

Makes 8 to 10 servings (about 5 quarts).

SATISFYING FULL-MEAL SOUPS

Spanish Bean and Sausage Soup

Served with a basket of cherry tomatoes, French rolls with butter, and an unpretentious red wine, *caldo gallego* makes a satisfying meal. For dessert, dot fresh fruit—such as papaya, pineapple, or halved bananas—with butter and brown sugar; then broil until golden.

1 pound (about 2½ cups) dried small white beans, rinsed and drained

2 quarts water

2 smoked ham hocks (about 1½ lbs)

1 large onion, finely chopped

2 stalks celery, with leaves, finely chopped

1 large clove garlic, minced or pressed

2 medium potatoes (about 1 lb), diced

2 small turnips (about ½ lb), peeled and diced

4 small chorizo sausages (about ¾ lb)

1 bunch (about 12 oz) spinach

Salt (optional)

Cilantro (Chinese parsley), for garnish

1. Place beans in a large bowl; add 2 teaspoons salt and 6 cups water. Cover and let stand for at least 8 hours; drain, discarding soaking liquid. *Or*, to shorten the soaking period, place beans in a 3- to 4-quart pan with 2 quarts water (*no salt*); bring to boiling; then boil briskly, uncovered, for 2 minutes. Remove from heat, cover, and let stand for 1 hour. Drain, discarding soaking liquid.

2. In a 5- to 6-quart kettle, combine drained beans, the 2 quarts water, ham hocks, onion, celery, garlic, potatoes, and turnips. Bring to boiling over medium heat. Cover, reduce heat, and boil gently until beans are very tender (3½ to 4 hours).

3. Meanwhile, remove and discard sausage casings and slice sausages ½ inch thick. Cook sausages in their own drippings in a medium frying pan over moderate heat, stirring often, until lightly browned. Remove sausage with a slotted spoon, drain, and reserve.

4. Remove ham hocks from beans. When they are cool enough to handle, discard bones and skin; return ham in large chunks to soup. Add prepared sausage; cook, uncovered, stirring occasionally, for about 10 minutes.

5. Meanwhile, rinse and drain spinach. Remove and discard stems. Coarsely shred leaves; add to soup and cook, stirring, just until spinach is wilted and bright green. Taste, and add salt if needed.

6. Serve hot soup garnished with sprigs of cilantro.

Makes 6 to 8 servings (12 to 14 cups).

Swiss Lentil, Ham, and Vegetable Soup

Lentils cook more quickly than other dried legumes and make an appealing soup with vegetables and ham hocks. Serve the soup with a crusty light rye bread and beer, then berries with cream for dessert.

¼ cup dried mushrooms

Hot water

2 leeks

2 medium carrots, chopped

2 medium onions, slivered

1 stalk celery, thinly sliced

1 clove garlic, minced or pressed

2 tablespoons butter or margarine

10 cups water

1 pound dried lentils (about 2½ cups), rinsed and drained

1 medium potato (about ½ lb), finely diced

1 large tomato, peeled and chopped

4 smoked ham hocks (2½ to 3 lbs)

¾ cup chopped fresh parsley

¼ teaspoon white pepper

1 teaspoon mustard seed, crushed

1 bay leaf

Salt (optional)

2 hard-cooked eggs, shredded

1. Place mushrooms in a small bowl and cover with hot water; let stand until soft (30 minutes to 1 hour).

2. Meanwhile, cut off root ends of leeks; remove and discard coarse outer leaves. Cut off and discard green tops so that leeks are about 9 inches long. Split lengthwise, from leafy end, cutting to within about 1 inch of root end. Soak in cold water for several minutes; then separate leaves under running water to rinse away any clinging grit; drain. Slice about ¼ inch thick.

3. In a 6- to 8-quart kettle over medium heat, cook leeks, carrots, onions, celery, and garlic in butter, stirring often, until soft but not browned.

4. To vegetables add the 10 cups water, lentils, potato, tomato, ham hocks, ½ cup of the parsley, pepper, mustard seed, and bay leaf. Bring to boiling. Meanwhile, drain mushrooms and chop coarsely; add to lentil mixture. When it begins to boil, cover, reduce heat, and simmer until ham is very tender (3 to 3½ hours).

5. Remove and discard bay leaf. Remove ham hocks. Purée about 2 cups of the lentils and vegetables in blender or food processor; then return to soup. When ham hocks are cool enough to handle, discard bones and skin; return ham in large chunks to soup. Taste, and add salt if needed. Reheat if necessary.

6. Serve hot, garnishing each serving with hard-cooked egg and some of the remaining ¼ cup chopped parsley.

Makes 6 servings (about 14 cups).

Cranberry Bean Minestrone

If you shop in a neighborhood with an Italian heritage, you may have seen fresh cranberry beans in the markets in September and October. Sold in pods flecked with cranberry red, they need to be shelled before cooking. Though fresh, the beans still take a fair amount of time to cook—half to three-quarters of an hour or longer.

This colorful soup takes advantage of the special character of these beans. If you can't find them, however—or in another season—you can make the soup using 2 cups of other cooked dried red or white beans, or drained canned kidney or pinto beans.

Serve the soup with thick slices of Italian bread, red wine, and for dessert, fresh pineapple flavored with a little kirsch.

1½ pounds fresh cranberry beans

1 pound mild Italian pork sausages

2 tablespoons olive oil

1 large onion, finely chopped

1 large carrot, cut lengthwise in quarters, then thinly sliced

Thick split pea soup made with both ham and sliced frankfurters is a dish brimming with Black Forest gemütlichkeit.

Split Pea Soup, Black Forest Style

Add fresh parsley and sliced green onions just before you serve this tangy pea soup dotted with veal frankfurter slices. Accompany it with a light rye bread, a red and green cabbage slaw with a sour cream dressing, and tart red apples for dessert. Beer or, better yet, an Alsatian Gewürztraminer is a good beverage to go with the soup.

2 medium onions, finely chopped

2 medium carrots, diced

1 stalk celery, thinly sliced

2 tablespoons butter or margarine

1 medium potato (about ½ lb), diced

1 large smoked ham hock (about 1 lb) *or* **a meaty ham bone**

1 package (12 oz; about 1⅔ cups) green split peas, rinsed and drained

1 can or bottle (12 oz) beer

6 cups water

1 teaspoon dried thyme

2 teaspoons whole mustard seed, crushed

⅛ teaspoon ground cloves

½ pound veal frankfurters, sliced ½ inch thick

2 tablespoon cider vinegar

Salt (optional)

¼ cup *each* **chopped fresh parsley and sliced green onions**

1. Cook onions, carrots, and celery in heated butter in a 5½- to 6-quart kettle over medium heat, stirring occasionally, until vegetables are soft but not browned.

2. Add potato, ham hock, split peas, beer, water, thyme, mustard seed, and cloves. Bring to boiling, cover, reduce heat, and simmer until ham and peas are very tender (2 to 2½ hours), stirring occasionally.

3. Remove ham hock. When it is cool enough to handle, remove and discard bones and skin. Return meat to soup in large chunks.

4. Add frankfurter slices and reheat to serving temperature. Blend in vinegar. Taste, and add salt if needed. Stir in parsley and green onions, and serve at once.

Makes 6 servings (about 12 cups).

---

1 stalk celery, thinly sliced

1 large clove garlic, minced or pressed

1 sweet red or green bell pepper, seeded and chopped

¼ cup chopped fresh parsley

1 teaspoon dried basil

½ teaspoon dried oregano

¼ teaspoon dried marjoram

1 large can (about 30 oz) tomatoes packed in tomato sauce

3½ cups Sturdy Beef Broth (see page 8) *or* **2 cans (14½ oz** *each***) regular-strength beef broth**

½ cup dry red wine

¼ cup tiny soup pasta (*pastina***)**

1 quart coarsely shredded fresh spinach leaves

Salt (optional)

Grated Parmesan cheese

1. Split bean pods and slip out beans as if shelling peas. (You should have about 2 cups beans.)

2. Remove casings from sausages and crumble meat into heated oil in a 5- to 6-quart Dutch oven over medium heat. Brown sausage lightly, stirring often. Mix in onion, carrot, and celery; cook, stirring often, until onion is soft. If drippings are excessive, spoon off and discard most of the fat.

3. Add shelled beans, garlic, bell pepper, parsley, herbs, tomatoes (coarsely chopped) and their liquid, and broth. Bring to boiling, cover, reduce heat, and boil gently until beans are nearly tender (30 to 40 minutes).

4. Stir in wine and pasta and boil gently, uncovered, until pasta is tender (10 to 12 minutes). Add spinach, stirring just until it is wilted. Taste, and add salt if needed.

5. Serve with Parmesan cheese to sprinkle over each serving to taste.

Makes 4 to 6 servings (12 to 14 cups).

SATISFYING FULL-MEAL SOUPS

Start off an Italian dinner with apéritifs and a buttery tuna spread to go on herbed toast rounds. Then serve the robust Minestrone Milanese. Conclude with fruit, cheeses, and crisp nut cookies with espresso.

Crostini, crisp little toasts with a topping, are a favorite Italian first course with such apéritifs as Campari, Cynar, or vermouth. Usually the spread is a purée of savory chicken livers, but for this menu it is a tuna mixture.

The minestrone is smoky with ham and thick with rice in the style of Milan. For wine, select a light Zinfandel or a California or Italian Grignolino.

Cheeses that are particularly nice with pears or figs are Taleggio (a creamy Brie-like soft cheese), rich Fontina, and nutty (not too dry) Parmesan. The chewy cookies, known as *quaresimali* in Italy, are good with the coffee.

Tuna Toasts

1 large can (12½ oz) oil-packed tuna, drained

1 cup (½ lb) butter or margarine

½ cup whipping cream

1 teaspoon Dijon mustard

1 small dried hot red chile, finely crushed

¼ teaspoon coarsely ground black pepper

2 tablespoons chopped capers

¼ cup chopped fresh parsley

½ cup chopped pimiento-stuffed olives

Salt (optional)

Herbed Sourdough Thins (see page 54), thinly sliced French bread, or crackers

1. Place tuna in food processor. Cut butter in pieces and add to tuna with cream, mustard, chile, and pepper. Process until mixture is smooth.

2. Turn into a bowl and blend in capers, parsley, and ¼ cup of the olives. Taste, and add salt if needed. Spread in a crock or terrine. Cover and refrigerate until mixture is firm and flavors are well blended (2 to 3 hours or overnight).

3. Remove from refrigerator about ½ hour before serving. Garnish with remaining chopped olives and serve with Herbed Sourdough Thins.

Makes about 3½ cups.

Minestrone Milanese

1 cup dried cannellini or Great Northern beans, rinsed and drained

2½ to 3 pounds beef shanks, sliced ¾ to 1 inch thick

2 tablespoons olive oil

2 large onions, slivered

2 large carrots, chopped

2 stalks celery, thinly sliced

2 cloves garlic, minced or pressed

½ cup chopped fresh parsley

1 smoked ham hock (about ¾ lb)

1 large can (28 oz) tomatoes

2 tablespoons dried basil

2 quarts water

1 medium turnip, peeled and diced

2 cups chopped chard leaves

½ cup shelled fresh or frozen peas

1½ cups hot cooked rice

2 cups shredded cabbage

Salt (optional)

Grated Parmesan cheese

1. Place beans in a large bowl; add 1 teaspoon salt and 3 cups water. Cover and let stand for at least 8 hours; drain, discarding soaking liquid. *Or,* to shorten the soaking period, place

beans in a 2- to 3-quart pan with 1 quart water (*no salt*); bring to boiling; then boil briskly, uncovered, for 2 minutes. Remove from heat, cover, and let stand for 1 hour. Drain, discarding soaking liquid.

2. In a 7- to 8-quart kettle, brown beef shanks on both sides in heated olive oil over medium heat. As you turn shanks to brown the second side, add onions around them; cook, stirring occasionally, until onions are limp.

3. Add carrots, celery, garlic, parsley, ham hock, tomatoes (coarsely chopped) and their liquid, basil, drained soaked beans, and the 2 quarts water. Bring to boiling, cover, reduce heat, and simmer until meats and beans are tender (3½ to 4 hours). Skim and discard surface fat if necessary.

4. Remove beef shanks and ham hock with a slotted spoon. When cool enough to handle, discard bones and skin. Return beef and ham in large chunks to soup. (At this point, soup may be covered and refrigerated until ready to reheat and serve; skim fat from surface before reheating.)

5. Add turnip to soup and boil gently, uncovered, for 10 minutes. Mix in chard and peas and cook for 3 minutes more. Blend in rice and cabbage and cook, stirring occasionally, just until cabbage is wilted and bright green (3 to 5 minutes). Taste, and add salt if needed.

6. Serve with Parmesan cheese to sprinkle over each serving.

Makes 8 to 10 servings (about 5½ quarts).

Spiced Nut Cookies

2½ cups all-purpose flour

1½ teaspoons baking powder

1 teaspoon ground cinnamon

½ teaspoon ground nutmeg

¼ teaspoon *each* salt and ground allspice

¼ cup butter or margarine, softened

1 cup sugar

1 teaspoon vanilla

3 eggs

1 cup *each* unblanched whole filberts or almonds and coarsely chopped walnuts

⅓ cup pine nuts

Sugar for sprinkling

1. In a medium bowl, stir together flour, baking powder, cinnamon, nutmeg, salt, and allspice to blend well.

2. In a large bowl, beat butter with the 1 cup sugar until well combined. Blend in vanilla. Separate 1 of the eggs, reserving the white in a small bowl. To butter mixture add the 1 egg yolk, then the remaining whole eggs, one at a time, beating after each addition until smooth.

3. Gradually add flour mixture to butter mixture, mixing until smooth and well blended. Divide dough in half and wrap each portion in plastic wrap; refrigerate until firm (about 1 hour). Meanwhile, mix filberts, walnuts, and pine nuts.

4. On a lightly floured board or pastry cloth, roll out each portion of dough to an 8- by 12-inch rectangle. Sprinkle half of the nuts over each portion. Starting with a long side of each rectangle, roll dough to make a compact roll; pinch edge and ends to seal. Place, sealed side down, on a lightly greased baking sheet.

5. Beat the reserved egg white until slightly bubbly and brush generously over each roll. Sprinkle rolls lightly with sugar.

6. Bake in a 350°F oven until golden brown (35 to 40 minutes). Remove from oven and let rolls cool on baking sheet for about 5 minutes.

7. Transfer rolls to a board and use a serrated knife to slice each loaf diagonally into ½-inch-thick slices. Place slices, cut sides down, on baking sheets and bake again in 350°F oven until crisply toasted (15 to 20 minutes). Cool on racks.

Makes about 4 dozen cookies.

Red Beans, Ribs, and Hot Sausage Pot

Hot Louisiana-style sausage lights the flavor fire of this hearty, chili-like soup. You can vary the quantity of sausage as indicated to make the soup hot or hotter, as you prefer. With the soup, munch on crisp soda crackers and drink ice-cold beer.

1½ cups dried small red beans, rinsed and drained

2 to 2½ pounds country-style spareribs

2 tablespoons salad oil

2 large onions, finely chopped

1 stalk celery, thinly sliced

1 medium carrot, shredded

2 cloves garlic, minced or pressed

1 green pepper, seeded and chopped

1 bay leaf

½ teaspoon dried oregano

¼ teaspoon pepper

6 cups water

¾ to 1 pound Louisiana hot sausages

1 can (1 lb) tomatoes

Salt (optional)

2 to 3 tablespoons red wine vinegar

1. Place beans in a large bowl; add 1 teaspoon salt and 3 cups water. Cover and let stand for at least 8 hours; drain, discarding the soaking liquid. *Or*, to shorten the soaking period, place beans in a 2- to 3-quart pan with 1 quart water (*no salt*); bring to boiling; then boil briskly, uncovered, for 2 minutes. Remove from heat, cover, and let stand for 1 hour. Drain, discarding soaking liquid.

2. In a 5½- to 6-quart kettle, brown spareribs on all sides in heated oil over medium heat, removing ribs as they brown. (Do not crowd pan.) When all ribs are browned, add onions to same pan and cook, stirring often, until lightly browned. Mix in celery, carrot, garlic, green pepper, bay leaf, oregano, and pepper.

3. Return browned ribs to pan. Add drained beans and the 6 cups water. Bring to boiling, cover, reduce heat, and simmer until meat is tender (about 3 hours). Remove spareribs from pan; when they are cool enough to handle, return meat to pot in large chunks, discarding bones and fat. (At this point, soup may be covered and refrigerated until the next day if you wish.) Skim off and discard surface fat from soup.

4. Remove casings from sausages; cut in 1-inch chunks. Add to soup with tomatoes (coarsely chopped) and their liquid. Return soup to medium heat and bring slowly to boiling; then cover, reduce heat, and simmer until beans are tender and soup is thick (about 1 hour). Taste, and add salt if needed. Season to taste with vinegar.

5. Serve hot.

Makes 6 to 8 servings (about 4 quarts).

Scotch Broth

Chunky bone-in lamb neck or shoulder makes this barley and vegetable soup a substantial repast. Plan to start a day in advance. Serve it with a crusty whole-grain bread and butter, and a light red wine if you wish.

½ **cup pearl barley**

3 **pounds bone-in lamb neck, in large chunks**

2 **tablespoons butter or margarine**

1 **large onion, finely chopped**

2 **cloves garlic, minced or pressed**

1 **sweet red or green bell pepper, seeded and chopped**

2 **medium carrots, chopped**

1 **small celery root (about ½ lb), peeled and finely chopped**

1 **bay leaf**

1 **teaspoon salt**

¼ **teaspoon** *each* **white pepper and dried thyme**

   Pinch ground allspice

2 **quarts water**

¼ **cup chopped fresh parsley**

1. Place barley in a small bowl, cover with water, and let stand for 8 hours or overnight.

2. Meanwhile, brown lamb pieces on all sides, about half at a time, in heated butter in a 5½- to 6-quart kettle over medium heat, removing lamb as it browns. To same kettle, add onion and cook, stirring occasionally, until soft. Mix in garlic, bell pepper, carrots, and celery root. Return lamb to pot; then add bay leaf, salt, white pepper, thyme, allspice, and the 2 quarts water. Bring to boiling, cover, reduce heat, and simmer until lamb is very tender (2½ to 3 hours).

3. Remove chunks of lamb from soup. Remove and discard bay leaf. When lamb is cool enough to handle, remove and discard bones and fat. Return meat to soup in large chunks. Cover and refrigerate for several hours or overnight.

4. Skim and discard fat from soup. Drain soaked barley and add it to the soup. Bring soup slowly to boiling, stirring occasionally; then cover, reduce heat, and boil gently until barley is tender (45 minutes to 1 hour).

5. Taste, and add salt if needed. Stir in parsley and serve at once.

Makes 6 servings (about 12 cups).

Plan ahead to make Scotch Broth, an inspired assemblage of winter vegetables, barley, and lamb. The soup is best if it is chilled, then skimmed before you finish cooking it.

Old-Fashioned Navy Bean Soup

Good accompaniments for this traditional, thick soup are a crisp coleslaw, corn muffins, and a luscious homemade dessert such as a peach pie.

1 **pound (about 2½ cups) dried small white beans, rinsed and drained**

2 **quarts water**

4 **smoked ham hocks (2½ to 3 lbs)**

1 **large onion, finely chopped**

1 **bay leaf**

3 **whole cloves**

½ **teaspoon sugar**

2 **stalks celery, with leaves, finely chopped**

1 **carrot, shredded**

⅛ **teaspoon white pepper**

   Salt (optional)

1. Place beans in a large bowl; add 2 teaspoons salt and 6 cups water.

Cover and let stand for at least 8 hours; drain, discarding soaking liquid. *Or,* to shorten the soaking period, place beans in a 3- to 4-quart pan with 2 quarts water (*no salt*); bring to boiling; then boil briskly, uncovered, for 2 minutes. Remove from heat, cover, and let stand for 1 hour. Drain, discarding soaking liquid.

2. In a 5- to 6-quart kettle, combine drained beans, the 2 quarts water, ham hocks, onion, bay leaf, cloves, sugar, celery, carrot, and pepper. Bring to boiling over medium heat. Cover, reduce heat, and boil gently until beans are very tender and soup begins to thicken (4 to 5 hours).

3. Remove and discard bay leaf. Remove ham hocks. When they are cool enough to handle, discard bones and skin; return ham in large chunks to soup. Taste, and add salt if needed.

4. Reheat, if necessary, and serve soup hot.

Makes 6 servings (about 10 cups).

SATISFYING FULL-MEAL SOUPS

Chicken and Turkey Soups

One of the few bright spots during inflationary times has been the price of chicken—amazingly, it remains reasonable. This versatile bird can be the economical star of many kinds of dishes, not the least of which is soup.

Without making claims as to the medicinal value of chicken soup, one can say that such good fare as the chicken soups that follow is certainly a tonic for lagging appetites or spirits.

Turkey, too, can be counted among the truly good buys for your grocery dollar. Sold ground or in parts, it is appealing in soups as well as many other dishes.

Chicken and Tortellini Soup

Tortellini, the fetchingly shaped (one Italian legend has it that they were modeled after the navel of Venus) stuffed pasta, combine with chicken drumsticks in this quick soup. If you can't get tortellini, you might substitute plain, unsauced ravioli.

4 *each* **chicken legs and thighs (2¼ to 2½ lbs)**

2 tablespoons olive oil

2 medium onions, slivered

1 stalk celery, thinly sliced

2 medium carrots, chopped

1 large clove garlic, minced or pressed

1 teaspoon dried basil

½ teaspoon dried oregano

¼ teaspoon *each* dried thyme and sage

1 large can (28 oz) tomatoes

1¾ cups Rich Chicken Broth (see page 9) *or* 1 can (14½ oz) chicken broth

1 cup dry red wine

1 can (8 oz) tomato sauce

1 package (12 oz) frozen tortellini

Boiling salted water

3 cups slivered chard or spinach leaves (discard coarse stems)

Salt (optional)

Grated Parmesan cheese

1. In a 4½- to 5-quart Dutch oven, brown chicken pieces, about half at a time, in heated olive oil over medium heat, removing them as they brown.

Pour off all but about 2 tablespoons of the drippings. To same pan, add onions, celery, and carrots. Cook, stirring often, until soft but not browned. Mix in garlic. Return chicken to pan.

2. Sprinkle with basil, oregano, thyme, and sage. Mix in tomatoes (coarsely chopped) with their liquid, broth, wine, and tomato sauce. Bring to boiling, cover, reduce heat, and simmer until chicken is tender and broth is flavorful (about 1 hour).

3. Meanwhile, cook tortellini in boiling salted water according to package directions. Rinse with cold water, drain well, and reserve.

4. Mix cooked tortellini and slivered chard into soup and cook, uncovered, until chard is wilted and bright green and tortellini are heated (3 to 5 minutes). Taste, and add salt if needed.

5. Serve in broad, shallow bowls with Parmesan cheese to sprinkle over each serving to taste.

Makes 4 to 6 servings (about 15 cups).

Majorcan Chicken and Sausage Soup

Serve this Spanish soup with a salad of greens, oranges, and red onions, and a light red wine or Mexican beer.

2 tablespoons olive oil

1 medium carrot, shredded

1 large onion, thinly slivered

1 stalk celery, thinly sliced

1 clove garlic, minced or pressed

A 3- to 3½-pound chicken, cut up (including giblets)

Pinch saffron threads

1 teaspoon salt

1 can (1 lb) tomatoes

6 cups water

½ pound chorizo sausages

¼ cup tiny star-shaped pasta

¼ cup coarsely chopped cilantro (Chinese parsley) or fresh parsley

Tempting Chicken and Tortellini Soup needs only bread and a green salad to make a full meal. Frozen tortellini are often available at Italian grocery stores and delicatessens.

1. Heat olive oil in a 4- to 5-quart kettle over moderate heat; then add carrot, onion, and celery. Cook, stirring often, until onion is soft but not browned. Mix in garlic.

2. Add chicken pieces (including neck, heart, and gizzard; reserve liver to cook later) and sprinkle with saffron and salt. Add tomatoes (coarsely chopped) with their liquid and the water. Bring to boiling, cover, reduce heat, and simmer until chicken is very tender and broth is flavorful (2 to 2½ hours).

3. Remove chicken pieces; discard bones and skin, and separate meat into large chunks. Chop heart and gizzard finely. (You can do this much ahead; wrap and refrigerate the meat, and cover and refrigerate the soup.) Skim off and discard fat from surface of broth.

4. Shortly before serving soup, remove sausage casings and slice chorizos about ¼ inch thick. Brown lightly in a medium frying pan in sausage drippings. Remove from pan and drain on paper towels, reserving drippings.

5. Bring soup slowly to boiling over medium heat. Add pasta and the browned sausage and cook, uncovered, until pasta is nearly tender (10 to 12 minutes). Meanwhile, cut chicken liver in half and brown quickly in reserved sausage drippings. Cut liver pieces into ¼-inch-wide strips.

6. Return chicken to soup and cook until heated through (about 5 minutes). Mix in liver strips. Taste, and add salt if needed.

7. Stir in cilantro and serve at once.

Makes 4 to 6 servings (10 to 12 cups).

Provençal Chicken Soup

Fresh fennel flavors this handsome chicken soup. The part of the fennel to use is the lower, bulb-shaped portion of each feathery-fronded stalk. If fennel is not available, increase the celery to two stalks, and add ⅛ teaspoon fennel or anise seed (finely crushed). Serve the soup with French bread, crisp radishes on a bed of ice, and a light red wine.

1 leek

2 tablespoons olive oil

2 medium carrots, chopped

1 medium onion, finely chopped

1 stalk celery, thinly sliced

½ cup chopped fresh fennel

1 clove garlic, minced or pressed

A 3- to 3½-pound chicken, cut up (reserve giblets for other uses)

½ cup chopped fresh basil leaves *or* 2 tablespoons dried basil

1 teaspoon salt

⅛ teaspoon white pepper

7 cups water

¼ teaspoon saffron threads

3 medium tomatoes, peeled, seeded, and chopped

1 tablespoon anise-flavored apéritif (such as Pernod or Ricard), optional

1. Cut off root end of leek; remove and discard coarse outer leaves. Cut off and discard green top so that leek is about 9 inches long. Split lengthwise from leafy end, cutting to within about 1 inch of root end. Soak in cold water for several minutes; then separate leaves under running water to rinse away any clinging grit; drain. Slice about ¼ inch thick.

2. Heat olive oil in a 4- to 5-quart kettle over moderate heat; then add leek, carrots, onion, celery, and fennel. Cook, stirring often, until onion is soft but not browned. Mix in garlic. Add chicken pieces; then sprinkle with half of the basil and the salt and pepper. Add water. Bring to boiling, cover, reduce heat, and simmer until chicken is very tender and broth is flavorful (2 to 2½ hours).

3. Remove chicken pieces; discard bones and skin, and separate meat into large chunks. (You can do this much ahead; wrap and refrigerate meat, and cover and refrigerate soup.) Skim off and discard fat from surface of broth.

4. Bring soup slowly to boiling over medium heat. Remove about ⅓ cup of the broth and stir saffron into it; let stand for 5 minutes. Add tomatoes and remaining basil to soup; then add saffron mixture. Return chicken to soup and cook until heated through (about 5 minutes). Taste, and add salt if needed.

5. Blend in apéritif and serve at once.

Makes 6 servings (11 to 12 cups).

Curried Turkey Soup

An array of colorful garnishes—hard-cooked eggs, toasted coconut, and green onions—accents this quick-cooking ground-turkey soup. Serve it with a salad of sliced cucumbers in yogurt, an Indian flatbread or warm cracker bread, and beer or iced tea.

1½ pounds ground turkey, crumbled

3 tablespoons butter or margarine

1 large onion, finely chopped

4 teaspoons curry powder

½ teaspoon mustard seed, crushed

1 medium carrot, shredded

1 tart green apple, peeled, cored, and shredded

2 cloves garlic, minced or pressed

6 cups Rich Chicken Broth (see page 9) *or* 3 cans (14½ oz *each*) chicken broth

1 cup whipping cream

½ cup shelled fresh or frozen peas

2 egg yolks

1 teaspoon grated lemon peel

Salt (optional)

Sieved hard-cooked egg, toasted shredded coconut, and thinly sliced green onions, for garnish

1. In a 3½- to 4-quart saucepan over medium heat, cook turkey in heated butter, stirring often, until it loses its pink color. Add onion, curry powder, and mustard seed; cook, stirring often, until onion is soft. Mix in carrot, apple, and garlic.

2. Add broth. Bring slowly to boiling, cover, reduce heat, and simmer for 40 minutes.

3. Add cream and peas and cook, uncovered, over medium heat until mixture is steaming and heated through (about 5 minutes). Beat egg yolks in a small bowl. Blend in a little of the hot soup; then blend egg yolk mixture into soup. Stir constantly over low heat until soup begins to thicken. (Do not boil.) Stir in lemon peel. Taste, and add salt if needed.

4. Serve with small bowls of sieved egg, coconut, and green onions to garnish each serving to taste.

Makes 6 servings (about 12 cups).

Turkey Garbure

Garbure, a soup of long-standing tradition in the Southwest of France, is usually made with duck or goose. In these weight-conscious times, turkey is a lighter choice—and it is more easily come by, too. Turkey teams well with such time-honored ingredients as dried white beans, turnips, and cabbage. Serve this lusty soup with a rough, country-style bread, sliced or cherry tomatoes, and a red jug wine.

- **1 cup small white beans, rinsed and drained**
- **3 leeks**
- **2 medium onions, chopped**
- **2 tablespoons butter or margarine**
- **3 cloves garlic, minced or pressed**
- **1 teaspoon *each* dried thyme and marjoram**
- **¼ teaspoon white pepper**
- **1 large smoked ham hock (1 to 1½ lbs) *or* a meaty ham bone**
- **2½ to 3 pounds turkey drumsticks or thighs**
- **3 medium potatoes (1 to 1¼ lbs), diced**
- **3 medium carrots, sliced**
- **3 small turnips, cut in quarters, then sliced**
- **½ cup chopped fresh parsley**
- **1 bay leaf**
- **10 cups water**
- **1 small cabbage (about 1 lb), cut into thin wedges**
- **3 tablespoons red wine vinegar**
- **Salt (optional)**

1. Place beans in a large bowl; add 1 teaspoon salt and 3 cups water. Cover and let stand for at least 8 hours; drain, discarding soaking liquid. *Or,* to shorten the soaking period, place beans in a 2- to 3-quart pan with 1 quart water (*no salt*); bring to boiling; then boil briskly, uncovered, for 2 minutes. Remove from heat, cover, and let stand for 1 hour. Drain, discarding soaking liquid.

2. Cut off root ends of leeks; then cut off green tops so that leeks are about 9 inches long. Remove coarse outer leaves. Rinse well to remove grit. Slice about ¼ inch thick.

3. In a 7½- to 8-quart kettle, cook leeks and onions in melted butter over medium heat, stirring often, until soft but not browned. Stir in garlic, thyme, marjoram, and pepper. Then add drained beans, ham hock, turkey, potatoes, carrots, turnips, parsley, bay leaf, and the 10 cups water. Bring slowly to boiling; then cover, reduce heat, and simmer until beans and turkey are very tender (3½ to 4 hours).

4. Remove and discard bay leaf. Remove turkey and ham hock from soup. Scoop out about 3 cups beans and vegetables with a little broth. When turkey and ham are cool enough to handle, remove meat in chunks and return it to soup; discard bones, skin, and fat. Skim and discard surface fat from soup. Purée bean mixture in blender or food processor until smooth; return it to soup.

5. Stir soup over medium heat until it boils gently. Add cabbage and gently stir occasionally, uncovered, until cabbage is tender and bright green (8 to 10 minutes).

6. Blend in vinegar; then taste, and add salt if needed. Serve hot.

Makes 10 to 12 servings (about 6 quarts).

Winter Avocado Feast

Guacamole with Crisp Raw Vegetables and Corn Chips

Mexican Chicken and Avocado Soup

Warm Corn Bread   Butter

Berry Sherbet

Pecan Polvorones

Beer   Coffee

When an abundance of winter avocados makes them an affordable luxury, schedule this menu for six that showcases the fruit in two courses. Start with your favorite guacamole to scoop up with either crisply fried tortilla triangles or an assortment of carrot and celery sticks, thin turnip slices, and radishes.

The soup, in the style of the seaside resort of Ixtapa, also features avocados. Add the slices just before you serve the soup—too much heat makes avocado taste bitter.

The cookies are typical of the treats sold in Oaxacan bakeries; they taste delicious with a tart fruit ice.

Mexican Chicken and Avocado Soup

- **A 3- to 3½-pound chicken, cut up (reserve giblets for other uses)**
- **1 stalk celery, thinly sliced**
- **2 medium carrots, chopped**
- **2 medium onions, slivered**
- **1 large clove garlic, minced or pressed**
- **1 teaspoon *each* salt and whole cumin seed, crushed**
- **½ teaspoon dried oregano**
- **2 small dried red chiles, crushed**
- **6 cups water**
- **2 cups cut green beans (fresh or frozen)**
- **2 medium tomatoes, seeded and chopped**
- **¼ cup chopped fresh cilantro (Chinese parsley)**
- **1 large avocado, peeled, seeded, and thinly sliced**
- **Lime wedges, for garnish**

1. In a 5- to 6-quart kettle or Dutch oven, combine chicken, celery, carrots, onions, garlic, salt, cumin seed, oregano, chiles, and water. Bring slowly to boiling; then cover, reduce heat, and simmer until chicken is very tender and broth is flavorful (2 to 2½ hours).

2. Remove chicken pieces; discard bones and skin, and separate meat into chunks. (You can do this much

SATISFYING FULL-MEAL SOUPS

ahead; wrap and refrigerate meat, and cover and refrigerate soup.) Skim and discard fat from surface of broth.

3. Bring soup to boiling, add green beans, and cook, uncovered, for 5 minutes. Add chicken, reduce heat, and cook until it is heated through (3 to 5 minutes). Taste, and add salt if needed. Mix in tomatoes, cilantro, and avocado slices.

4. Serve with lime wedges to squeeze into each portion of soup to taste.

Makes 6 servings (about 12 cups).

Pecan Polvorones

½ cup (¼ lb) butter or
    margarine, softened

½ cup lard, at room
    temperature

¾ cup sugar

1 egg yolk

1 teaspoon vanilla

2¼ cups all-purpose flour

½ teaspoon ground cinnamon

    Pinch salt

½ cup finely chopped pecans

    Additional granulated sugar

1. In a large bowl, cream butter and lard with the ¾ cup sugar until fluffy. Beat in egg yolk and vanilla until well combined.

2. In another bowl, stir together flour, cinnamon, and salt to blend well. Gradually add flour mixture to creamed mixture, beating until well combined. Blend in pecans.

3. To form each cookie, shape dough into a ball the size of a small walnut; roll in granulated sugar to coat generously. Place cookies on ungreased baking sheets. Using a glass dipped in sugar, flatten each cookie to a thickness of about ½ inch.

4. Bake in a 350°F oven for 10 minutes; then reduce heat to 300°F and continue baking until cookies are lightly browned (12 to 15 minutes). Let cool slightly (hot cookies break easily); then remove to wire racks to cool completely.

Makes about 3 dozen cookies.

Celebrate avocados with this menu featuring them in two forms: as a guacamole dip for crisp vegetables and corn chips and as a last-minute addition to a vivid Mexican chicken soup. For dessert, bring on berry sherbet and meltingly tender sugar cookies.

Minted Chicken and Garbanzo Soup

The hot flavor of red chile and the cool contrast of fresh mint are an intriguing match in a chicken soup that may well trace its origins to the cooking of the Near East.

- **1 cup dried garbanzos (ceci beans or chick-peas), rinsed and drained**
- **2 tablespoons olive oil or salad oil**
- **1 large onion, finely chopped**
- **1 stalk celery, thinly sliced**
- **2 cloves garlic, minced or pressed**
- **1 bay leaf**
- **1 small dried hot red chile, crushed**
- **½ cup chopped fresh mint leaves *or* 2 tablespoons dried mint**
- **6 cups water**
- **A 3- to 3½-pound chicken, cut up (reserve giblets for other uses)**
- **1 large can (28 oz) tomatoes**
- **Salt (optional)**

1. Place beans in a bowl; add 1 teaspoon salt and 3 cups water. Cover and let stand for at least 8 hours; drain, discarding soaking liquid. *Or,* to shorten the soaking period, place beans in a 2- to 3-quart pan with 1 quart water (*no salt*); bring to boiling; then boil briskly, uncovered, for 2 minutes. Remove from heat, cover, and let stand for 1 hour. Drain, discarding soaking liquid.

2. Heat oil in a 5½- to 6-quart kettle or Dutch oven; add onion and celery and cook over medium heat, stirring often, until soft but not browned. Mix in garlic, bay leaf, crushed chile, and half of the mint; then add drained beans and the 6 cups water. Bring to boiling, cover, reduce heat, and boil gently for 1 hour.

3. Add chicken pieces and tomatoes (coarsely chopped) and their liquid. Return to a gentle boil, cover, reduce heat, and simmer until chicken and beans are tender (about 2 hours).

4. Remove chicken pieces and let cool slightly; remove meat in chunks, discarding bones and skin. Set aside.

5. Scoop out about 2 cups of the cooked beans and tomatoes with a little of the cooking liquid. Place in blender or food processor and whirl or process until smoothly puréed. Mix

into soup; then add chicken. Taste, and add salt if needed.

6. Reheat soup to serving temperature. Blend in remaining fresh or dried mint, stir for about 1 minute, and serve soup hot.

Makes 6 servings (12 to 14 cups).

Chicken and Potato Soup Piccante

Lavish Cheddar cheese over this chicken soup, and serve it with sesame-sprinkled homemade muffins, crisp raw vegetables, and beer.

- **1 medium onion, finely chopped**
- **1 sweet red bell pepper, seeded and chopped**
- **1 stalk celery, thinly sliced**
- **2 tablespoons butter**
- **1 clove garlic, minced or pressed**
- **1 can (4 oz) diced green chiles**
- **4 medium-size, smooth-skinned potatoes (1½ to 2 lbs), diced**
- **A 3- to 3½-pound chicken, cut up (reserve giblets for other uses)**
- **½ teaspoon dried thyme**
- **1 teaspoon salt**
- **7 cups water**
- **Shredded Cheddar cheese, for garnish**

1. Cook onion, bell pepper, and celery in melted butter in a 5- to 6-quart kettle over medium heat, stirring occasionally, until onion is soft but not browned.

2. Mix in garlic, green chiles, and potatoes. Add chicken pieces. Sprinkle with thyme and salt. Add water. Bring slowly to boiling, cover, reduce heat, and simmer until chicken is very tender and broth is flavorful (2 to 2½ hours).

3. Remove chicken pieces; discard bones and skin, and separate meat into chunks.

4. Scoop out about 2 cups of vegetables from soup with a little of the broth; purée in blender or food processor until smooth. Return purée to soup. Skim and discard surface fat. Add chicken and cook, occasionally stirring gently, until heated through. Taste, and add salt if needed.

5. Serve hot soup with cheese to sprinkle over each serving to taste.

Makes 6 servings (about 12 cups).

Chicken and Meatball Soup

All you could want to accompany this satisfying chicken soup are sourdough bread and butter, a glass of white wine, and perhaps a ruffly salad of young greens.

- **A 3- to 3½-pound chicken, cut up (reserve giblets for other uses)**
- **1 stalk celery, thinly sliced**
- **1 large carrot, chopped**
- **1 large onion, finely chopped**
- **1 teaspoon salt**
- **1 bay leaf**
- **½ teaspoon dried thyme**
- **¼ teaspoon dried sage**
- **7 cups water**
- **Veal and Pork Meatballs (recipe follows)**
- **Grated Parmesan cheese**

1. In a 5- to 6-quart kettle or Dutch oven, combine chicken, celery, carrot, onion, salt, bay leaf, thyme, sage, and water. Bring slowly to boiling; then cover, reduce heat, and simmer until chicken is very tender and broth is flavorful (2 to 2½ hours).

2. Remove chicken pieces; discard bones and skin, and separate meat into large chunks. (You can do this much ahead; wrap and refrigerate meat, and cover and refrigerate soup.) Skim and discard fat from surface of broth.

3. Bring soup slowly to boiling over medium heat. Add meatballs, about 8 at a time, and cook, uncovered, until meatballs come to the surface. Cover and simmer for 5 minutes. Then add chunks of chicken to soup and cook just until meat is heated through. Taste, and add salt if needed.

4. Serve in broad, shallow bowls with Parmesan cheese to sprinkle over each serving to taste.

Makes 6 servings (about 12 cups).

Veal and Pork Meatballs In a medium bowl, beat 1 egg; mix in ¼ cup *each* soft bread crumbs and grated Parmesan cheese, ¾ teaspoon salt, ¼ teaspoon dried marjoram, a pinch of ground nutmeg, and 1 small clove garlic (minced or pressed). Lightly mix in ¼ cup finely chopped fresh parsley and ½ pound *each* ground veal and ground pork. Shape into 1-inch meatballs.

Three Ways to Make Chinese Chicken Soup

A fragrantly steaming bowl of soup is a favorite opener for a Chinese meal. On tasting these subtle flavors and brilliantly colored tidbits, many Westerners wish they could make an entire meal of such a soup.

Although it may not be traditional, there is no reason not to do just that. Here is a recipe for a basic chicken soup that can be turned into your choice of colorful Chicken Corn Soup, peppery Hot-and-Sour Soup, or dramatic Sizzling Rice Soup. This is a more substantial soup than you will find in a Chinese restaurant (where just the meaty bones of chicken used in other dishes flavor the broth).

Sizzling Rice Soup gets its name from the addition of the dry crust that forms on the bottom of the rice pot. However, you can also cook rice and then dry it in the oven before frying.

Chicken Corn Soup is just one variation you can make from a basic Chinese soup.

Chinese Chicken Soup

A 3- to 3½-pound chicken, cut up (discard giblets)

2 slices (about ¼ inch thick) peeled ginger root, slivered

3 green onions, chopped

1 clove garlic, sliced

1 teaspoon salt

6 cups water

Ingredients for Chicken Corn Soup, Hot-and-Sour Soup, *or* Sizzling Rice Soup (recipes follow)

1. In a 5- to 6-quart kettle, combine chicken, ginger, green onions, garlic, salt, and water. Bring slowly to boiling; then cover, reduce heat, and simmer until chicken is very tender and broth is flavorful (2 to 2½ hours).

2. Remove chicken pieces; discard bones and skin, and dice or shred meat. Strain broth, discarding seasonings. (You can do this much ahead; wrap and refrigerate meat, and cover and refrigerate soup.) Skim and discard fat from surface of broth.

3. Proceed with one of the three following variations.

Chicken Corn Soup Reheat broth in kettle over medium heat. Add ¼ teaspoon Chinese chile oil (see Note) and 1 medium carrot (quartered lengthwise, then thinly sliced). Cover and boil gently for 5 minutes. Stir in 1½ to 2 cups fresh corn kernels (cut from 2 medium ears) and ½ cup shelled fresh or frozen peas; cook, uncovered, for 3 minutes. Mix in cooked chicken. In a small bowl, blend 1 tablespoon cornstarch smoothly with 2 tablespoons water. Blend into soup, stirring until it boils and becomes clear. In a medium bowl, beat 2 eggs. Remove soup pan from heat. Add eggs slowly to soup, stirring constantly, until they form long threads. Taste, and add salt if needed. To serve, sprinkle soup with 3 tablespoons thinly sliced green onions.

Makes 6 servings (10 to 12 cups).

Hot-and-Sour Soup When cooking chicken and broth, add 1 small dried red Chinese chile (coarsely crushed; see Note) with ginger and green onions. Soak 4 large dried Chinese mushrooms (see Note) in warm water to cover for 30 minutes; drain and squeeze dry. Cut off and discard stems. Cut caps into thin slivers. Trim meat from 1 loin pork chop (¾ inch thick, about ½ lb); cut meat into long, thin strips.

Reheat broth in kettle over medium heat. Add sliced mushrooms and pork and ½ cup matchstick-sliced canned bamboo shoots. Cover and simmer for 10 minutes. Add cooked chicken, ½ cup diced tofu (see Note), and ¼ pound peeled tiny shrimp. Cook, uncovered, for 3 minutes. Stir in ¼ cup rice wine vinegar (see Note). In a small bowl, blend 1 tablespoon cornstarch with 1 tablespoon *each* soy sauce and water, ½ teaspoon Chinese chile oil (see Note), and ¼ teaspoon *each* white pepper and Oriental sesame oil (see Note). Blend cornstarch mixture into soup, stirring until it boils and becomes clear. In a medium bowl, beat 2 eggs slightly. Remove pan from heat. Add eggs slowly to soup, stirring constantly, until they form long threads. Taste, and add salt if needed. To serve, sprinkle soup with ⅓ cup thinly sliced green onions.

Makes 6 servings (10 to 12 cups).

Sizzling Rice Soup Bring 1½ cups water to boiling in a small pan; add ⅔ cup short-grain rice, cover, reduce heat, and simmer for 20 minutes. Remove pan from heat and let stand, covered, for 30 minutes. Then pat rice out evenly about ½ inch thick on a greased baking sheet. Dry in a 300°F oven until rice feels dry on surface (1 to 1½ hours). Break into irregular bite-size pieces. Set aside.

Reheat broth in kettle. Add 1 stalk celery (thinly sliced on the diagonal), 1 small onion (thinly slivered), ¼ cup sliced water chestnuts, and 1 cup sliced fresh mushrooms. Cover and boil gently for 5 minutes.

Meanwhile, pour salad oil into a deep, heavy frying pan or wok to a depth of 1 inch; heat to 375°F on a frying thermometer. Fry pieces of dried cooked rice, about half at a time, until golden brown (½ to 1 minute). Drain; keep warm on an ovenproof plate in a 300°F oven.

Snap off ends and remove strings from 1 cup edible-pod peas. Add to soup with cooked chicken; cook, uncovered, until chicken is heated (3 to 5 minutes). Blend in 1 tablespoon *each* soy sauce and dry sherry and 1 teaspoon Oriental sesame oil (see Note). Salt to taste. Ladle into a warm bowl.

Bring soup to table on a tray with warmed bowls and hot rice. Ladle soup into bowls; then add 2 or 3 pieces of hot fried rice to each.

Makes 6 servings (10 to 12 cups).

Note Oriental markets stock these items.

Soups with Fish

It used to be a bit of a joke to refer to men's formal wear as a soup-and-fish. When dinners followed a rigid pattern of set courses, dress was just that stiffly predictable.

None of the soups ahead can be described by such adjectives as *formal, rigid, stiff,* or *predictable.* They all entice with surprising, light-hearted flavors. You will find that the two creamy chowders require little time to prepare, yet each can be served as the centerpiece of a special—though unconventional—dinner.

Creamy Salmon Chowder

The flavors of a sumptuous baked salmon dish at Chef Alain Dutournier's Paris restaurant, Au Trou Gascon, inspired this suave salmon chowder. Serve it as a main course with a salad of mushrooms and young greens, followed by a nut ice cream and crisp cookies for dessert.

4 shallots, slivered (about ¾ cup)

3 tablespoons butter or margarine

1 teaspoon dried tarragon

3 medium-size, smooth-skinned potatoes (about 1½ lbs), thinly sliced

½ teaspoon salt

⅛ teaspoon white pepper

2 cups Fish Broth or Rich Chicken Broth (see page 9) *or* 1 can (14½ oz) chicken broth

1½ pounds salmon steaks, ¾ to 1 inch thick

1 lemon, thinly sliced

1 bay leaf

1 cup dry white wine

¼ pound sliced bacon, cut in ½-inch-wide pieces

Half a small cabbage, cored and thinly shredded (about 1 qt)

1 cup whipping cream

1. In a heavy 4- to 5-quart saucepan or Dutch oven, cook shallots in butter over medium heat, stirring, until soft but not browned. Mix in tarragon.

2. Add potatoes. Sprinkle with salt and pepper. Add broth and bring to boiling. Cover, reduce heat, and boil gently for 15 minutes.

3. Add salmon steaks in a single layer; cover with lemon slices; then add bay leaf. Pour in wine. Cover again and cook over low heat until salmon flakes when tested with a fork and potatoes are tender (10 to 12 minutes). Meanwhile, cook bacon in its own drippings in a medium frying pan until lightly browned. Remove from heat, drain, and keep warm.

4. Remove salmon steaks. Remove and discard bay leaf and lemon slices. Remove and discard salmon bones and skin and divide salmon into chunks. Add cabbage and cream to soup. Stir occasionally over medium heat until cabbage is wilted and bright green (3 to 5 minutes). Gently mix in salmon. Taste, and add salt if needed.

5. Serve chowder hot, spooning several pieces of bacon into each bowl.

Makes 4 to 6 servings (10 to 12 cups).

Warm Weather Soup Dinner

Tricolor Artichoke Salad

Sole in Mint Broth

French Bread   Butter

Creamy Lime Sherbet with Raspberries

White Wine   Coffee

Hot soup is certainly a welcome meal in cold weather, and when you plan carefully, it's also a good choice for a warm evening. Consider this menu for one of those unexpectedly sunbathed fall days when summer's warmth lingers.

A colorful salad starts you off, followed by an elegantly simple fish soup—small sole fillets poached in less than 5 minutes in a refreshingly minty broth.

If there are still fresh raspberries to be found, they are a delightful garnish for a homemade lime sherbet waiting in the freezer.

Tricolor Artichoke Salad

1 package (8 oz) frozen artichoke bottoms

1½ cups thinly sliced or coarsely chopped radishes

Creamy Mustard Dressing (recipe follows)

1 tablespoon snipped fresh chives or finely chopped green onions

6 cups torn romaine leaves

½ cup (about 3 oz) crumbled goat cheese (*chèvre*)

1. Cook artichoke bottoms according to package directions just until tender. Drain, rinse with cold water to stop cooking, and drain again.

2. Just before serving, mix radishes, half of the dressing, and chives in a small bowl. In another bowl, lightly mix romaine, remaining dressing, and goat cheese.

3. To serve, divide the romaine mixture among 4 salad plates. Arrange a fourth of the artichoke bottoms on each plate. Fill artichoke bottoms with radish mixture, dividing it evenly. Serve at once.

Makes 4 servings.

Creamy Mustard Dressing In a medium bowl, mix 1 egg yolk, 1½ tablespoons tarragon wine vinegar, 1½ teaspoons Dijon mustard, a pinch *each* salt and cayenne pepper, and 1 clove garlic (minced or pressed). Using a whisk or fork, slowly and gradually beat in ⅓ cup olive oil until dressing is thick and creamy. Makes about ½ cup.

Sole in Mint Broth

1 medium onion, thinly slivered

1 medium carrot, thinly sliced

2 tablespoons butter or margarine

1 lemon

1 small clove garlic, minced or pressed

¼ teaspoon white peppercorns

1 small bay leaf

½ teaspoon salt

Sole poached in a mint-flavored broth makes a soup refreshing enough to serve on a warm day, along with an artichoke salad.

1 cup dry white wine

3 cups Fish Broth or Rich Chicken Broth (see page 9) *or* canned chicken broth

1 pound small sole fillets

¾ cup coarsely chopped fresh mint leaves

1. In a large, deep frying pan, cook onion and carrot in butter over medium heat, stirring often, until soft but not browned.

2. Using a lemon stripper or small knife, remove peel from lemon in vertical strips. (Reserve strips to use in drinks if you wish.) Then cut lemon in half lengthwise and slice each half thinly.

3. Add lemon slices to onion mixture with garlic, peppercorns, bay leaf, salt, wine, and broth. Bring to boiling, cover, reduce heat, and simmer for 20 minutes.

4. Add fish fillets to liquid, cover, and cook gently over medium heat (liquid should barely bubble) for 2 minutes. Sprinkle with mint and continue cooking, uncovered, gently spooning broth over fish, just until fish is opaque and begins to separate into flakes when tested with a fork (2 to 3 minutes). Taste, and add salt if needed.

5. Use a slotted spoon to transfer fish fillets to warm, broad, shallow soup bowls. Ladle broth over them.

Makes 4 servings.

Creamy Lime Sherbet

4 large limes (about ¾ lb)
Lemon juice, if needed

2 cups half-and-half (light cream)

1 cup sugar

Few drops green food coloring (optional)

1. Grate lime peel; you should have about 3 tablespoons. Set aside. Squeeze limes and measure the juice. Add lemon juice, if needed, to make ½ cup.

2. In a medium bowl, stir half-and-half with sugar until sugar dissolves. Mix in lime peel and juice. Blend in food coloring to tint mixture a pale green if you wish. Freeze in a loaf pan until firm (3 to 4 hours).

3. Remove sherbet from freezer and break up with a spoon; then transfer to a bowl and beat with an electric mixer until fluffy. Place in a covered container, return to freezer, and freeze again until firm (several hours or overnight).

4. Scoop into chilled dishes to serve.

Makes about 3 cups.

Breton Mussel and Shrimp Soup with Rice

Cooking, cleaning, and shelling fresh mussels and shrimp for this crimson soup is a bit of a job, but once that is done, the rest goes together quickly. And the delicious results are well worth the work. Accompany the soup with a whole-grain bread, sweet butter, and a dry white wine such as Muscadet.

- **2 quarts (about 3 lbs) uncooked mussels in shells**
- **3 sprigs parsley**
- **¼ teaspoon white peppercorns**
- **2 cups dry white wine**
- **1 pound shrimp in shells, cooked (directions follow)**
- **Liquid from cooking mussels and shrimp**
- **1½ to 2 cups Fish Broth or Rich Chicken Broth (see page 9) or 1 can (14½ oz) chicken broth**
- **⅛ teaspoon saffron threads**
- **2 shallots, finely chopped**
- **1 medium onion, thinly slivered**
- **½ pound mushrooms, thinly sliced**
- **¼ cup butter or margarine**
- **1 clove garlic, minced or pressed**
- **⅛ teaspoon cayenne pepper**
- **1 can (6 oz) tomato paste**
- **Salt (optional)**
- **¼ cup chopped fresh parsley**
- **3 cups hot cooked rice**

1. Discard any mussels that may have opened. Clean mussels by scraping off any barnacles. Then scrub with a stiff brush under running water to remove sand; drain.

2. In a 4- to 5-quart kettle, combine mussels, parsley sprigs, peppercorns, and 1 cup of the wine. Bring to boiling over medium heat, cover, reduce heat, and simmer until mussels have opened (6 to 8 minutes). Discard any mussels that remain closed.

3. Remove mussels from liquid, reserving liquid. Reserve a few mussels in shells for garnish. Remove remaining mussels from shells. (You should have about 2 cups.) Pinch out and discard the ''beard'' from any mussel that has one. Peel and devein shrimp; add to mussels and set aside.

4. Strain mussel and shrimp cooking liquids through a dampened cloth. Measure the combined liquid. Add Fish Broth to make 6 cups.

5. Place saffron in a small bowl and add ¼ cup of the hot shellfish liquid. Set aside to steep.

6. In a 3½- to 4-quart pan, cook shallots, onion, and mushrooms in heated butter over medium heat, stirring often, until soft and lightly browned. Mix in garlic, cayenne, and tomato paste. Then add the shellfish liquid, saffron mixture, and remaining 1 cup white wine.

7. Bring slowly just to boiling, stirring occasionally, until soup is steaming hot. Mix in cooked mussels and shrimp. Taste, and add salt if needed. Mix in chopped parsley. Serve soup hot over rice in broad, shallow soup bowls. Garnish with mussels in shells.

Makes 6 servings (10 to 12 cups).

To cook shrimp In a 3- to 4-quart saucepan or Dutch oven, combine 1½ cups water, ½ cup dry white wine, 1 small onion (thinly sliced), 1 stalk celery (coarsely chopped), 1 bay leaf, 3 sprigs fresh parsley, 1 teaspoon salt, ¼ teaspoon black peppercorns, and 1 tablespoon lemon juice. Bring to boiling, cover, reduce heat, and simmer 5 minutes. Add 1 pound fresh shrimp in shells. When mixture returns to boiling, remove pan from heat, cover, and let stand 10 minutes. Drain shrimp, reserving liquid. Makes about 2 cups shrimp (with 2 cups liquid).

Cheese-Crusted Fish Soup

This thick, red fish soup with a broiled topping of toasted croutons and cheese synthesizes several *soupes de poissons* of the Atlantic coast of France. As a first course, try a green vegetable salad—asparagus, broccoli, or green beans in a vinaigrette dressing—and drink a light red wine with the soup.

- **1 medium onion, thinly slivered**
- **1 stalk celery, thinly sliced**
- **1 sweet red bell pepper, seeded and chopped**
- **3 tablespoons olive oil**
- **3 cloves garlic**
- **1 small dried hot red chile, crushed**
- **½ teaspoon *each* salt, dried thyme, and basil**

Not so long ago, finding fresh mussels was no easy job. Now that they are more available, enjoy them in this Breton soup with shrimp ladled over a mound of rice.

⅛ teaspoon anise or fennel seed, crushed

Pinch ground cloves

1 large can (28 oz) tomatoes

¼ cup tomato paste

2 cups Fish Broth or Rich Chicken Broth (see page 9) *or* 1 can (14½ oz) chicken broth

1 cup dry white wine

6 slices (about ½ inch thick) French bread

6 tablespoons grated Parmesan cheese

1 pound lingcod steaks

1 to 1½ pounds sea bass fillets, cut in 1-inch-wide strips

½ pound peeled tiny cooked shrimp

¼ cup chopped fresh parsley

2 cups (½ lb) shredded Swiss cheese

1. In a 4- to 5-quart kettle or Dutch oven, cook onion, celery, and bell pepper in olive oil over medium heat, stirring often, until onion is soft but not browned. Mince or press 2 of the garlic cloves and add to onion mixture with chile, salt, thyme, basil, anise seed, and cloves.

2. Mix in the tomatoes (coarsely chopped) and their liquid, tomato paste, broth, and wine. Bring to boiling, cover, reduce heat and simmer for 45 minutes.

3. Meanwhile, place bread slices on a baking sheet. Peel remaining clove of garlic, cut it in half, and with it rub both sides of each bread slice. Bake in a 325°F oven until crisp and lightly browned (40 to 45 minutes). Sprinkle each slice with 1 tablespoon of the Parmesan cheese.

4. Remove and discard skin and large central bone from each lingcod steak, cut fish in chunks, and add to soup. Simmer, uncovered, for 20 minutes. Then add sea bass fillets and shrimp. Cook over medium heat, uncovered, stirring occasionally, just until sea bass flakes when tested with a fork (3 to 5 minutes). Taste, and add salt if needed. Mix in parsley.

5. Divide soup among ovenproof bowls. Top each with a slice of toasted French bread. Divide Swiss cheese evenly over the bread. Place bowls on a baking sheet about 6 inches below broiler. Broil until cheese bubbles and browns lightly (6 to 8 minutes). Serve at once.

Makes 6 servings (about 12 cups).

Curried Scallop and Leek Soup

This rich golden soup is intended as a main dish, but in smaller servings it can also be served as a first course.

3 leeks

2 shallots, finely chopped

3 tablespoons butter or margarine

2 teaspoons curry powder

¼ teaspoon ground ginger

Pinch cayenne pepper

2 cloves garlic, minced or pressed

1 pound scallops (cut in halves if large)

3 cups Fish Broth or Rich Chicken Broth (see page 9) *or* canned chicken broth

1 cup whipping cream

2 egg yolks

2 tablespoons lemon juice

1 cup dry white wine

Salt (optional)

Thinly sliced green onions, for garnish

1. Cut off root ends of leeks; remove and discard coarse outer leaves. Cut off and discard green tops so that leeks are about 8 inches long. Split lengthwise, from leafy end, cutting to within about 1 inch of root end. Soak in cold water for several minutes; then separate leaves under running water to rinse away any clinging grit; drain. Slice about ¼ inch thick.

2. Cook leeks and shallots in melted butter in a 3- to 4-quart pan, stirring often over medium heat, until leeks are soft but not browned. Stir in curry powder, ginger, cayenne, and garlic.

3. Add scallops, broth, and cream. Bring slowly to the boiling point; then cover, reduce heat, and simmer until scallops are opaque in center (about 5 minutes). Do not overcook or scallops will become tough. Remove scallops with a slotted spoon; reserve them.

4. Beat egg yolks with lemon juice in a small bowl until blended.

5. Transfer mixture in which scallops cooked, about half at a time, to a blender or food processor, whirl or process until smooth, and return it to cooking pan. Blend wine into soup. Gradually add about ½ cup of the soup to egg yolk mixture, stirring to blend. Then add egg yolk mixture, all at once, to soup. Return scallops to soup. Stir over low heat until soup is

steaming hot. (*Do not boil.*) Taste, and add salt if needed.

6. Serve soup hot, garnished with a sprinkling of green onion slices.

Makes 4 servings (about 8 cups).

Red-and-White Fish Chowder

This colorful chowder is not difficult to prepare and goes together quickly. The Crisp Bread Sticks on page 54 are a good accompaniment.

1 large onion, thinly slivered

1 stalk celery, thinly sliced

1 sweet red bell pepper, seeded and chopped

¼ cup butter or margarine

½ teaspoon dried thyme

3 medium-size red-skinned potatoes (about 1½ lbs), scrubbed and diced (unpeeled)

½ teaspoon salt

⅛ teaspoon white pepper

2 cups Fish Broth or Rich Chicken Broth (see page 9) *or* 1 can (14½ oz) chicken broth

1½ pounds red snapper fillets, cut crosswise in 1-inch-wide strips

¼ pound sliced pancetta or bacon, cut in ½-inch-wide pieces

2 cups half-and-half (light cream)

1. In a heavy 3½- to 4-quart saucepan, cook onion, celery, and bell pepper in butter over medium heat, stirring until onion is soft but not browned. Mix in thyme.

2. Add potatoes. Sprinkle with salt and pepper. Add broth and bring to boiling. Cover, reduce heat, and boil gently for 15 minutes.

3. Add fish strips, cover again, and cook over low heat until fish flakes when tested with a fork and potatoes are tender (8 to 10 minutes). Meanwhile, cook pancetta in its own drippings in a medium frying pan until lightly browned. Remove from heat, drain, and keep warm.

4. Blend half-and-half gently into the soup and cook, stirring occasionally, just until soup is steaming hot. (*Do not boil.*) Taste, and add salt if needed.

5. Serve chowder hot, spooning several pieces of pancetta into each bowl.

Makes 4 to 6 servings (about 10 cups).

Home-Baked Soup Accompaniments

Soup and crackers is one of those pairings of foods that seem so right it's hard to think of one without the other. The two are natural and necessary opposites, the crispness of the cracker contrasting with the soup's smoothness. Packaged crackers and flatbreads are to be found in ever-expanding, tempting variety, but they can also be made at home to complement your good soups.

Herbed Sourdough Thins are seasoned, toasted slices from a long, slender loaf. Nutlike Whole Wheat Squares are a savory sort of graham cracker. The Italian-style bread sticks, or *grissini*, make a good match with soups, stews, or pasta. Break apart oversize rounds of Armenian Cracker Bread, or *lahvosh*, after they are baked and cooled to make irregular shards that invite nibbling.

Herbed Sourdough Thins

A 15-inch-long sourdough baguette (about ½ lb)

3 tablespoons *each* butter or margarine and salad oil

1 teaspoon lemon juice

1 clove garlic, minced or pressed

½ teaspoon freeze-dried chives

¼ teaspoon *each* paprika and dried savory

½ cup grated Parmesan cheese

1. Thinly slice bread crosswise. (You should have about 48 slices.) Arrange in a single layer on baking sheets.

2. Melt butter with oil in a small pan over medium heat. Add lemon juice and bring to boiling, stirring; boil for 1 minute. Mix in garlic and remove from heat. Stir in chives, paprika, and savory.

3. Brush bread slices lightly and evenly with butter mixture. Sprinkle evenly with Parmesan cheese.

4. Bake in a 300°F oven until crisp and lightly browned (30 to 35 minutes).

5. Serve hot, or let cool on wire racks and serve at room temperature. If Sourdough Thins are made more than 24 hours in advance, wrap tightly and freeze; then spread on a baking sheet and heat in a 300°F oven for about 10 minutes before serving.

Makes about 4 dozen slices.

Whole Wheat Squares

1 egg

¾ cup milk

2 cups whole wheat flour

1 cup all-purpose flour

¼ cup wheat germ

1 teaspoon *each* salt and baking powder

6 tablespoons butter or margarine

Coarse salt (optional)

1. In a small bowl, beat egg with milk. In a large bowl, mix flours, wheat germ, salt, and baking powder. Cut in butter until mixture resembles coarse crumbs. Gradually blend in egg mixture, mixing until dough pulls away from sides of bowl.

2. Divide dough into 2 portions. With flour-dusted hands, pat each portion out on a greased 12- by 15-inch baking sheet to a rectangle about ½ inch thick. With a floured rolling pin, roll dough out evenly to edges of pan. Use a pastry wheel or pizza cutter to mark dough into about 2-inch squares. Sprinkle lightly with coarse salt if you wish. Pierce with a fork at about 1-inch intervals.

3. Bake in a 325°F oven until lightly browned (25 to 30 minutes).

4. Let crackers cool on wire racks; then carefully break apart.

Makes about 8 dozen crackers.

Crisp Bread Sticks

1 package active dry yeast

⅔ cup warm water

¼ cup olive oil

1 teaspoon salt

1 tablespoon sugar

2¼ to 2½ cups unbleached all-purpose flour

1 egg, lightly beaten with 1 teaspoon water

Sesame seed

1. Sprinkle yeast over warm water in large bowl of electric mixer. Let stand until softened (about 5 minutes).

2. Add olive oil, salt, sugar, and 1¼ cups of the flour. Mix to blend; then beat at medium speed until smooth and elastic (about 5 minutes). Then gradually beat in about 1 cup more flour to make a stiff dough.

3. Turn dough onto a floured board

or pastry cloth and knead until dough is springy and small bubbles form just beneath surface (5 to 10 minutes). Transfer to a greased bowl, cover, and let stand in a warm place until dough doubles in bulk (about 1 hour).

4. Punch dough down and divide in half. Cut each half of the dough into 15 equal pieces. Using palms of hands, roll each piece on a floured surface to a stick about 12 inches long. Place about ¾ inch apart on greased baking sheets. Brush lightly with egg mixture; sprinkle with sesame seed. Let rise until puffy (30 to 35 minutes).

5. Bake in a 325°F oven until golden (25 to 30 minutes). Cool on racks.

Makes 30 bread sticks.

Armenian Cracker Bread

2 eggs

1 cup milk

4 to 4½ cups all-purpose flour

1½ teaspoons *each* sugar and salt

¼ cup vegetable shortening

4 teaspoons sesame seed

1. Beat eggs with milk in a small bowl.

2. In a large bowl, mix 4 cups of the flour, the sugar, and salt. Cut in shortening until mixture resembles coarse crumbs. Gradually blend in egg mixture, mixing until dough pulls away from sides of bowl.

3. On a floured board or pastry cloth, knead dough lightly to form a smooth ball. Divide the dough into 4 parts; wrap 3 of them in plastic wrap to keep them from drying out. Work with and bake one portion at a time.

4. On the floured surface, roll out dough until it is about ⅛ inch thick. Add flour as needed to prevent dough from sticking. Re-form into a ball; then roll out again to a circle about 14 inches in diameter.

5. Transfer carefully to a greased baking sheet or pizza pan. Brush lightly with water; then sprinkle with 1 teaspoon of the sesame seed.

6. Place a shallow pan of hot water on bottom rack of a 450°F oven. Place baking sheet on rack above it and bake bread for 3 minutes. Remove water, reduce heat to 300°F, and bake until bread is blistered, feels dry to the touch, and is lightly browned (12 to 15 minutes). Cool on a wire rack.

7. Repeat rolling and baking with remaining portions of dough.

8. When rounds of bread are crisp and cool, break apart to serve.

Makes 4 cracker breads, each 13 to 14 inches in diameter.

Breads to enhance soups: flat Armenian Cracker Bread, Herbed Sourdough Thins, Whole Wheat Squares, and Crisp Bread Sticks.

sk good cooks to describe their favorite dinners, and you will notice how proud most are of a certain kind of dish. Whether it's chicken, patiently marinated and browned, then lovingly simmered in wine; or beef in a savory, bubbling broth; or fork-tender lamb garlanded with spring vegetables, there is a common denominator. In each instance the cook is talking about a stew.

Many of the world's great dishes are stews—meat or poultry, which may or may not be browned first, cooked slowly in a well-seasoned liquid until it is tender, moist, and irresistible. Every country has at least one stew that could be considered a national dish—indeed, a national treasure. Italy gives us *bollito misto*; the Philippines, *adobo*; and France has several candidates, among them *coq au vin*.

In the southwestern United States, chili is the stew cooks strive to perfect. Recipes for three entrants in the chili sweepstakes can be found on pages 66–67.

Whatever your preference in stews, you will generally find them a good choice for a special meal. Choose one of these abundant kettles for a dinner when all the family gathers to celebrate an occasion, or when you want to share a convivial evening with a group of friends.

Most of these stews require a fair amount of cooking time. But usually once you have them safely simmering, you can ignore them while you attend to other matters. Split-second timing is rarely essential—if a stew has to wait an extra half hour, it won't go to pieces. Before you plan to freeze a stew to serve at a later date, review the tips on pages 6–7.

French Cocotte of Beef, Mushrooms, and Wine (the recipe is on page 60), marinated for as much as a day before cooking, makes an elegant stew for a special dinner.

Meaty Stews

Abundant in beef, veal, pork, lamb, or variety meats, all these stews are substantial and also have a certain finesse. Many use thrifty cuts of meat, so in serving them for a dinner party you may find that you have invested more time than money in their preparation.

When a recipe calls for cut-up meat, don't automatically reach for the so-called stew meat—already cubed—in the meat case. First have a look at a similar boneless whole roast; if the price per pound is less, it is probably worth your while to perform the simple task of cutting it in pieces in your own kitchen.

Bolognese Boiled Dinner

A dazzling array of meats and vegetables, each added at just the right stage to achieve tenderness, makes up the Italian simmered dinner known as *bollito misto*. A piquant green sauce unites all the elements. If you wish, serve the broth in which everything cooked as a first course, or strain and freeze it to become the cooking medium for your next *bollito misto*.

Look for the distinctive, plump *coteghino* sausage in Italian delicatessens; if it isn't stocked regularly, perhaps the dealer can order it for you. It contributes a lot of flavor to the dish.

A 3½- to 4-pound beef rump roast

3 quarts water *or* Sturdy Beef Broth (see page 8)

1 fresh beef tongue (2½ to 3 lbs)

1 veal shank (1 to 1½ lbs), cut through bone into 3 sections

1 large onion, finely chopped

4 large carrots

2 stalks celery, sliced

5 sprigs parsley

1 tablespoon salt

¼ teaspoon *each* whole allspice and black peppercorns

A 1- to 1½-pound *coteghino* sausage (optional)

4 to 6 leeks, well rinsed, with coarse outer leaves discarded and leafy tops trimmed to about 5 inches

10 to 12 small red potatoes, scrubbed (unpeeled)

1 small Savoy (curly) cabbage (about 1 lb), cut into 8 wedges

Green Sauce (recipe follows)

Bolognese Boiled Dinner features meats, sausage, and vegetables with Green Sauce.

1. Place roast in a shallow roasting pan. Bake, uncovered, in a 500°F oven, turning once, until well browned (20 to 25 minutes). Transfer to a 10- to 12-quart kettle. Add a little of the water to pan, stirring to loosen brown drippings; pour over roast.

2. To roast, add tongue, veal shank, and onion. Slice 1 of the carrots and add it to meats with celery, parsley, salt, allspice, peppercorns, and remaining water. Bring to boiling over medium heat, cover, reduce heat, and simmer for 2 hours.

3. Add sausage, cover again, and cook for 1 hour more. Meanwhile, cut 3 remaining carrots lengthwise into quarters; cut quarters crosswise into halves. Add to kettle with leeks and potatoes; cook until meats and potatoes are tender (about 45 minutes).

4. With a slotted spoon, remove tongue and set it aside. Remove roast, veal shank, and sausage to a large, warm platter. Surround with leeks, potatoes, and carrots. Cover lightly with foil and keep warm.

5. Cut off and discard bones and gristle at the thick end of the tongue. Slit the skin on the underside, and starting at the thick end, peel it off. Add tongue to meats and vegetables on platter.

6. Add cabbage to gently boiling broth and cook it, uncovered, until it is tender and bright green (8 to 10 minutes). Add to meats and vegetables on platter.

7. If you wish to serve broth as a first course, strain, salt if needed, and serve it hot.

8. Then carve meats and serve with vegetables and Green Sauce.

Makes 10 to 12 servings.

FESTIVE AND FILLING STEWS

Green Sauce In a blender or food processor, combine ½ cup olive oil, ¼ cup white wine vinegar, 3 green onions (coarsely chopped), 1 cup lightly packed fresh parsley, 2 tablespoons capers, 1 clove garlic (minced or pressed), 1 tablespoon anchovy paste, a pinch of pepper, and ¼ cup lightly packed fresh basil leaves (or 1 tablespoon dried basil). Whirl or process until smoothly blended. Taste, and add salt if needed. Serve at room temperature. Makes about 1¼ cups.

Tangy Pot Roast Stew

When people talk about the wonders of their mother's (or grandmother's) cooking, the conversation usually comes around to pot roast. If your mother comes from the region of Emilia-Romagna in Italy, perhaps this is the way she cooked it. The rich, brown sauce is good with homemade pasta or other noodles.

A 3½- to 4-pound blade-cut or seven-bone chuck roast, fat trimmed

2 tablespoons olive oil

2 red onions, slivered

1 package (12 oz) fresh baby carrots, scrubbed and trimmed (unpeeled)

1 stalk celery, thinly sliced

2 cloves garlic, minced or pressed

1 teaspoon salt

¼ teaspoon *each* ground cloves and coarsely ground pepper

½ teaspoon dried thyme

1 cup Sturdy Beef Broth (see page 8) *or* canned regular-strength beef broth

2 tablespoons balsamic vinegar or red wine vinegar

Chopped parsley, for garnish

1. Brown roast well on both sides in heated oil in a large, deep frying pan over medium heat or an electric frying pan on medium setting; remove and reserve pot roast. Spoon off and discard all but about 2 tablespoons of drippings. Add onions, carrots, and celery, and cook, stirring, until onions brown lightly. Mix in garlic.

2. Sprinkle both sides of browned roast with mixture of salt, cloves, pepper, and thyme. Place roast on top of vegetables in pan. Pour broth over roast; drizzle with vinegar. Cover, reduce heat, and simmer until meat is very tender (2½ to 3 hours).

3. Remove roast to a warm platter or board. Remove and discard bones, dividing roast into several large sections. Slice each section across the grain. Remove vegetables with a slotted spoon and place them around roast. Cover lightly with foil to keep warm.

4. Skim and discard surface fat from cooking liquid. Bring to boiling, stirring, until it is reduced and slightly thickened. Sprinkle pot roast with chopped parsley and serve with sauce.

Makes 4 to 6 servings.

Viennese Simmered Dinner

This combination of simmered beef and hearty vegetables has an Austrian accent. In the essay collection *Blue Trout and Black Truffles*, the late Joseph Wechsberg explains, "Few Americans think of boiled beef as the gastronomic treat it is known for in Central Europe." He then goes on to say, "In Vienna only the very best beef was good enough to be boiled."

For this presentation, choose the cone-shaped muscle of the blade chuck that when separated out as a roast is variously called chuck tender, mock tender, Scotch tender, or Jewish fillet. If this small boneless roast is not available, use fresh brisket.

Like *bollito misto*, this recipe produces two dishes: a creamy first-course soup and the sliced beef with a fluffy horseradish sauce for the main course.

A 3-pound chuck fillet roast or fresh brisket

6 cups water

2 leeks

3 medium carrots, thinly sliced

1 medium parsnip or turnip, peeled and finely chopped

1 small celery root (½ to ¾ lb), peeled and finely chopped

1 small onion, finely chopped

1 teaspoon salt

⅛ teaspoon white pepper

3 sprigs parsley

6 small new potatoes (1 to 1¼ lbs)

⅛ teaspoon paprika

½ cup whipping cream

Finely chopped fresh parsley, for garnish

Horseradish Cream Sauce (recipe follows)

Sour pickles and sharp mustard

1. Place beef in a shallow roasting pan. Bake, uncovered, in a 500°F oven, turning once, until well browned (15 to 20 minutes). Transfer to a 5½- to 6-quart kettle. Add a little of the water to roasting pan, stirring to loosen brown drippings; pour over roast.

2. Cut off root ends of leeks; remove and discard coarse outer leaves. Cut off and discard green tops so that leeks are about 8 inches long. Split lengthwise, from leafy end, cutting to within about 1 inch of root end. Soak in cold water for several minutes; then separate leaves under running water to rinse away any clinging grit; drain. Slice about ¼ inch thick.

3. To roast, add leeks, carrots, parsnip, celery root, onion, salt, pepper, parsley, and remaining water. Bring to boiling, cover, reduce heat, and simmer for 2½ hours.

4. Add potatoes and continue cooking until beef is very tender (30 minutes to 1 hour). Remove meat and potatoes from kettle and reserve them.

5. Strain broth, reserving vegetables. Measure 3 cups of the broth and return remainder to kettle over low heat. Return beef and potatoes to broth, cover, and keep warm until ready to serve.

6. Combine the 3 cups broth and reserved vegetables from broth (about half of each at a time) in blender or food processor. Whirl or process until smooth. Transfer to a 2½- to 3-quart saucepan and blend in paprika and cream. Stir over medium heat until soup is steaming hot. Taste, and add salt and white pepper if needed. Serve as a first-course soup.

7. Then arrange warm beef and potatoes on a board or warm platter. Slice beef thinly across the grain to serve. Drizzle with a little of the remaining broth. Sprinkle with parsley and accompany with Horseradish Cream Sauce, pickles, and mustard. Freeze remaining broth to use in other soups and stews in place of beef broth.

Makes 6 servings.

Horseradish Cream Sauce In a medium bowl, combine ½ cup whipping cream, ¼ teaspoon *each* sugar and dry mustard, and ½ teaspoon lemon juice. Beat until stiff. Fold in 2 tablespoons prepared horseradish. Cover and refrigerate for 1 to 3 hours to blend flavors. Makes about 1 cup.

Cocotte of Beef, Mushrooms, and Wine

The capacious saucepan in which this French stew simmers gives the dish its name. Marinated in red wine with herbs for as long as a day ahead of cooking, it will remind you of a *boeuf à la bourguignonne*. Serve it with traditional accompaniments—tiny new potatoes cooked in their jackets, buttered carrots, and a robust red wine.

3 pounds lean beef (chuck or rump), cut in 1-inch cubes

¼ cup brandy

2 tablespoons olive oil

2 medium onions, thinly slivered

2 cloves garlic, minced or pressed

1 teaspoon salt

½ teaspoon *each* sugar, peppercorns, juniper berries, and dried thyme

⅛ teaspoon *each* whole cloves and ground nutmeg

1 bay leaf

1½ cups dry red wine

3 tablespoons butter or margarine

½ pound large mushrooms, quartered

1 cup Sturdy Beef Broth (see page 8) *or* canned regular-strength beef broth

1 tablespoon tomato paste

1 tablespoon cornstarch blended with 2 tablespoons beef broth or water

Chopped fresh parsley, for garnish

1. Place cubed beef in a large, deep bowl; mix lightly with brandy and 1 tablespoon of the oil. Add onions, garlic, salt, sugar, peppercorns, juniper berries, thyme, cloves, nutmeg, and bay leaf. Pour in wine, mixing beef lightly with seasonings. Cover and refrigerate for 8 to 24 hours. Remove beef and onions from marinade, reserving marinade; pat beef dry.

2. In a heavy 4- to 5-quart saucepan or Dutch oven, heat remaining 1 tablespoon oil with butter over medium heat until butter melts. Brown mushrooms, removing them as they brown.

3. Brown beef well, a third to a half at a time, in same pan, removing cubes as they brown. Cook onions until limp. Return browned beef and

mushrooms to pan. Add broth and tomato paste. Strain marinade, discarding seasonings. Add marinade to beef mixture. Bring to boiling, cover, reduce heat, and simmer until meat is very tender (2 to 2½ hours).

4. Using a slotted spoon, remove beef and mushrooms to a warm serving dish and keep warm. Skim and discard fat from cooking liquid. Bring liquid to boiling over high heat, stirring, and cook until it is reduced by about a fourth. Remove from heat and blend in cornstarch mixture. Cook, stirring often, until thickened and clear. Taste, and add salt if needed.

5. Pour sauce over beef and mushrooms. Garnish with a sprinkling of parsley.

Makes 6 servings.

Braised Short Ribs with Peppers

Here is another savory beef dish of Italian origin. Red and green peppers give the abundant sauce substance and also garnish the cooked dish colorfully. Serve the ribs with noodles or butter-sautéed potato chunks.

3½ to 4 pounds English-cut beef short ribs, cut in serving pieces

Salt and coarsely ground pepper

2 tablespoons *each* olive oil and butter or margarine

2 large onions

2 teaspoons dried basil

½ teaspoon dried rosemary

1 medium carrot, shredded

1 stalk celery, finely chopped

2 *each* sweet red and green bell peppers

1 large clove garlic, minced or pressed

1 can (8 oz) tomato sauce

1 cup dry red wine

3 tablespoons rum (optional)

1. Sprinkle short ribs with salt and pepper. Brown on all sides, about half at a time, in 1 tablespoon *each* olive oil and butter in a large, deep frying pan or Dutch oven over medium heat. Remove ribs as they brown.

2. After ribs are browned, spoon off all but about 2 tablespoons of the drippings. To same pan, add 1 of the onions (chopped), 1 teaspoon of the basil, ¼ teaspoon of the rosemary, the

carrot, and the celery. Remove seeds from peppers and chop 1 red and 1 green pepper; add to onion mixture in pan. Cook, stirring, until onions are soft but not browned. Mix in garlic.

3. Return browned short ribs to pan. Blend in tomato sauce and wine. Bring to boiling, cover, reduce heat, and simmer until short ribs are very tender (2½ to 3 hours).

4. About 20 minutes before short ribs finish cooking, thinly sliver remaining onion and peppers. Heat remaining 1 tablespoon *each* olive oil and butter in a large frying pan over moderate heat. Add onion and cook, stirring often, until limp. Mix in peppers and remaining basil and rosemary. Continue cooking until onions brown lightly and peppers are tender-crisp (10 to 12 minutes). Remove from heat and keep warm.

5. Remove short ribs to a warm, deep platter and cover lightly to keep warm. Skim and discard fat from liquid in which short ribs cooked. Purée cooking liquid in blender or food processor; then add rum (if used) and reheat to serve. Taste, and add salt if needed. Pour sauce over short ribs; then spoon sautéed onion-and-pepper mixture over and around them.

Makes 8 servings.

Flemish Beef and Onions in Beer

In Belgium, where brewing is a finely developed craft, beer is the choice for cooking beef to tenderness. This stew uses a rump roast in one piece; after browning, it is simmered in a deep casserole in the oven. Serve it over fluffy potatoes that have been cooked, then mashed, with a bit of shredded carrot for color. If you would like to carry out the Belgian theme, add braised endive as a vegetable.

A 4- to 5-pound boneless rump roast

1 tablespoon *each* butter or margarine and salad oil

1 teaspoon salt

¼ teaspoon coarsely ground pepper

¾ teaspoon dried rosemary, crumbled

1 pound small white boiling onions, peeled

2 tablespoons red wine vinegar

1 tablespoon tomato paste

1 clove garlic, minced or pressed

Tangy sorrel, cooked with the veal, then puréed to make the sauce, flavors this stew. The recipe was inspired by a blanquette de veau *Jean-Paul Lacombe serves at his restaurant, Léon de Lyon. You might add a gratin of potatoes, such as the one on page 87.*

Creamy Veal Stew with Sorrel

Sorrel resembles spinach, but its flavor is much more acidic and lemony. Greengrocers who specialize in herbs and unusual lettuces are likely to have sorrel in the spring. Or you can grow some in your garden as readily as spinach.

   1 **bunch (3 or 4) leeks**
   ¼ **cup butter or margarine**
   1 **bunch (about 6 oz) sorrel, stems removed**
   3 **pounds boneless veal shoulder, cut in 1½-inch cubes**
   1 **teaspoon** *each* **salt and Dijon mustard**
   ¼ **teaspoon white pepper**
   1 **cup dry white wine**
   ½ **cup whipping cream**
   8 **green onions, with about 1½ inches of the leafy tops**
   8 **large mushroom caps**

1. Prepare leeks as in recipe for Viennese Simmered Dinner (see page 59).

2. Melt 2 tablespoons of the butter in a large, deep frying pan or Dutch oven over medium heat. Add sliced leeks and cook, stirring often, until limp but not browned. Cut about half of the sorrel leaves crosswise into ½-inch slivers; mix into leeks and cook until wilted and bright green. Mix in veal, salt, mustard, pepper, wine, and cream.

3. Bring to boiling, cover, reduce heat, and simmer until veal is very tender (about 1½ hours). With a slotted spoon, remove veal to a bowl and keep it warm.

4. Transfer cooking liquid to a blender and purée until smooth. Return purée to cooking pan and bring to boiling over high heat. Cook, uncovered, stirring often, until reduced by about half.

5. In remaining 2 tablespoons butter in a medium frying pan over moderate heat, cook green onions until bright green and just tender. (Do not brown.) Remove from pan and keep onions warm. In same pan, brown mushrooms lightly. Cut remaining sorrel in ¼-inch slivers.

6. To serve, taste sauce and season with salt if needed. Divide veal evenly among 4 warm plates. Pour sauce evenly over veal. Place 2 onions, green stems out, and 2 mushroom caps on each plate. Shower sorrel over veal. Serve at once.

Makes 4 servings.

   2 **bottles or cans (12 oz** *each*) **dark beer**
   2 **teaspoons Dijon mustard**
   1 **tablespoon all-purpose flour, creamed with 1 tablespoon soft butter or margarine**
   Additional vinegar (optional)
   Chopped fresh parsley, for garnish

1. Brown the roast on all sides in a mixture of heated butter and oil in a large frying pan over medium-high heat.

2. Reserving frying pan, place roast in a deep 3- to 5-quart covered casserole. Sprinkle with a mixture of salt, pepper, and rosemary. Surround with onions. Blend vinegar with tomato paste and garlic and drizzle over on-

ions. Pour out and discard fat from frying pan. To pan, add a little of the beer, stirring to dissolve brown drippings. Add drippings to casserole with remaining beer.

3. Cover and bake in a 350°F oven until the meat is very tender (4 to 4½ hours).

4. Spoon or pour cooking liquid into a large, deep frying pan. Keep meat and onions warm in casserole in turned-off oven. Bring liquid to boiling; then blend in first mustard, then bits of flour mixture, stirring until sauce is thickened. Taste, and add more vinegar if needed.

5. Slice meat thinly and arrange it on a warm, rimmed platter with onions around it. Spoon sauce over. Sprinkle with parsley.

Makes 8 to 10 servings.

Swiss Veal Shanks in White Wine Cream

Toss noodles with butter and a little grated Parmesan cheese to serve with these creamy veal shanks cooked with mushrooms. A green vegetable, such as beans or tiny peas, makes a nice contrast.

- **5 pounds meaty veal shanks, cut in about 2-inch slices**
- **Salt, white pepper, and nutmeg**
- **All-purpose flour**
- **4 to 6 tablespoons butter or margarine**
- **½ pound large mushrooms, quartered**
- **1 shallot, finely chopped**
- **1 clove garlic, minced or pressed**
- **½ teaspoon crumbled dried rosemary**
- **1 cup dry white wine**
- **½ cup Rich Chicken Broth (see page 9) or canned chicken broth**
- **1 cup whipping cream**
- **Grated lemon peel, for garnish**

1. Sprinkle veal shanks lightly with salt, pepper, and nutmeg. Dust with flour. Melt 4 tablespoons of the butter in a large, deep, heavy frying pan or 4½- to 5-quart Dutch oven over medium heat. Brown veal shanks, several at a time, removing them as they brown and adding more butter as necessary.

2. When all veal shanks are browned, add mushrooms and shallot to pan and brown lightly. Stir in garlic. Return veal shanks to pan and sprinkle with rosemary. Add wine and broth. Bring to boiling, cover, reduce heat, and simmer until veal is very tender (2 to 2½ hours).

3. Blend in cream, increase heat, and boil gently, uncovered, for 15 minutes. With a slotted spoon, remove veal shanks and mushrooms from liquid to a warm serving dish and keep warm.

4. Bring cooking liquid to boiling over high heat, stirring to incorporate browned bits in pan. Cook until sauce is slightly thickened and reduced; pour over veal. Sprinkle with grated lemon peel.

Makes 6 servings.

Garden-Fresh Dinner for Six

Sherried Artichoke Soup (see page 27)

Pot-Roasted Lemon Veal

New Potatoes

Dilled Carrot Purée   Garlic-Sautéed Zucchini

French Bread   Sweet Butter

Apple Tart Amandine

White Wine   Coffee

An abundance of fresh produce, both fruits and vegetables, accents this festive dinner. The smooth artichoke soup that gets the meal under way can be served hot or cold, depending on the weather.

Three vegetables—new potatoes, a creamy purée of carrots, and zucchini cut into matchsticks or slices and sautéed quickly in garlic butter—accompany the tender veal. The dessert tart mingles apples and almonds. A white wine such as a Meursault or Sancerre is a good choice with the main course.

Pot-Roasted Lemon Veal

- **A 3- to 3½-pound boned, rolled, and tied veal shoulder roast**
- **2 tablespoons butter or margarine**
- **1 tablespoon salad oil**
- **1 medium onion, chopped**
- **1 clove garlic, minced or pressed**
- **1 lemon**
- **1 medium carrot, sliced**
- **1 stalk celery, sliced**
- **4 sprigs parsley**
- **1 teaspoon salt**
- **¼ teaspoon white peppercorns**
- **⅛ teaspoon ground nutmeg**
- **1 cup dry white wine**
- **¾ cup whipping cream**
- **Flat-leaf parsley, for garnish**

1. Brown veal in mixture of heated butter and oil in a 4- to 5-quart Dutch oven or deep frying pan over medium heat until golden brown on all sides. As you turn roast to brown last side, add onion and garlic around edges, cooking and stirring occasionally until lightly browned.

2. Meanwhile, grate lemon peel and reserve it; squeeze juice from lemon. To browned veal, add lemon juice and all but 1 teaspoon of the lemon peel, the carrot, celery, parsley, salt, pep-

percorns, nutmeg, and wine. Bring to boiling, cover, reduce heat, and simmer until veal is very tender (1½ to 2 hours).

3. Remove roast to a warm, deep platter, cover lightly, and keep it warm. Strain and reserve cooking liquid, discarding solids. Return liquid to cooking pan and add cream.

4. Bring to boiling over high heat, stirring often. Cook and stir until sauce is slightly reduced and begins to thicken. Taste, and add salt if needed. Slice veal and arrange on platter. Pour sauce over. Garnish with reserved lemon peel and parsley.

Makes 6 servings.

Dilled Carrot Purée

- **6 medium carrots (about 1 lb), thinly sliced**
- **2 cups water**
- **¼ teaspoon each salt and dried dillweed**
- **¼ cup whipping cream**
- **2 tablespoons butter or margarine**
- **Pinch each ground nutmeg and white pepper**

1. In a 2-quart saucepan, combine carrots, water, salt, and dillweed. Bring to boiling over high heat; then cover, reduce heat, and boil gently until carrots are very tender (20 to 25 minutes).

Tender veal shoulder is cooked in wine with lemon, then sliced, sauced, and garlanded with vegetables to star in this elegant dinner.

2. Drain carrots well and transfer to a food processor or blender. Add cream and process or whirl until smooth. Return purée to cooking pan and place over low heat.

3. Blend in butter, nutmeg, and pepper. Stir until heated to serving temperature. Taste, and add salt if needed.

Makes 4 to 6 servings (about 1⅔ cups).

Apple Tart Amandine

Press-In Pastry (recipe follows)
5 large tart cooking apples (1¾ to 2 lbs)
2 eggs
⅓ cup sugar
¼ cup amaretto liqueur
Pinch salt
⅔ cup whipping cream

¼ cup sliced almonds
⅓ cup apricot preserves

1. Press pastry into bottom and up sides of an 11-inch removable-bottom tart pan.

2. Peel apples and cut in halves lengthwise; remove cores. Then cut each half in thin lengthwise slices, keeping slices together in apple shape. Arrange in prepared pastry shell, rounded sides up. After placing apple halves in shell, fan out slices slightly to cover most of the pastry.

3. In a medium bowl, beat eggs with sugar, amaretto, and salt until well combined. Blend in cream; pour evenly over apples. Sprinkle with almonds.

4. Bake in a 450°F oven for 15 minutes; reduce heat to 350°F and bake until filling is set and apples are tender

(50 minutes to 1 hour). Remove tart to a wire rack.

5. Stir preserves in a small pan over medium heat until melted and bubbling; strain to remove solid pieces of fruit. Brush glaze evenly over tart.

6. Remove pan sides and serve tart at room temperature.

Makes 1 pie (6 to 8 servings).

Press-In Pastry In a medium bowl, mix 1½ cups all-purpose flour and ¼ cup sugar. Cut in ½ cup (¼ lb) firm butter or margarine until crumbly. Beat 1 egg yolk with ½ teaspoon vanilla. With a fork, stir egg mixture lightly into flour mixture; then use your hands to press dough together into a smooth, flattened ball.

Bavarian Marinated Pork

Here, a pork loin roast gets the *Sauerbraten* treatment—marinating in wine with spices before it is braised. Try it with noodles and an off-dry white wine.

- **3 cups (750-ml bottle) off-dry or dry white wine**
- **2 medium onions, thinly sliced and separated into rings**
- **1 carrot, thinly sliced**
- **2 bay leaves**
- **1 teaspoon *each* whole cloves and slivered crystallized ginger**
- **1 tablespoon mixed pickling spices**
- **½ teaspoon *each* black peppercorns and dried thyme**
- **1 clove garlic, slivered**
- **½ cup apple cider vinegar**
- **A 3½- to 4-pound pork loin roast**
- **2 tablespoons butter or margarine**
- **1 tablespoon *each* sugar and tomato paste**
- **2 teaspoons salt**
- **¼ cup golden raisins**
- **2 tablespoons cornstarch, blended with 2 tablespoons water**

1. In a 2½- to 3-quart saucepan, heat together wine, onions, carrot, bay leaves, cloves, ginger, pickling spices, peppercorns, thyme, and garlic. Remove from heat and stir in vinegar. Pour over roast in a large, deep bowl. Cover and refrigerate for 24 to 48 hours, turning meat and stirring marinade occasionally.

2. Remove roast from marinade and pat dry; reserve marinade. Brown roast well on all sides in heated butter over medium heat in a 5½- to 6-quart Dutch oven. Spoon off excess fat. Pour in marinade. Blend in sugar, tomato paste, and salt. Bring to boiling, cover, reduce heat, and simmer until meat is very tender (2½ to 3 hours).

3. Remove meat to a warm platter, cover with foil, and keep warm. Strain cooking liquid, discarding seasonings and vegetables. Skim and discard surface fat from liquid. Return to Dutch oven, place over high heat, add raisins, bring to boiling, and boil until reduced by about a third.

4. Remove from heat and blend in cornstarch mixture. Boil, stirring constantly, until thickened and clear. Taste, and add salt if needed. Slice pork roast and serve accompanied by sauce.

Makes 6 to 8 servings.

Simmered Smoked Pork with Mustard-Glazed Onions

In the region of Alsace in eastern France, this traditional dish is called *schiffala*. After you have cooked the smoked pork shoulder roast to tenderness with wine and vegetables, add an innovative side dish: tiny onions cooked in some of the broth and then finished with mustard and cream. The combination is good with green beans (the tinier the better) and more of the Sylvaner. Strain the leftover broth, freeze it, and use it later to cook your favorite split pea, bean, or lentil soup.

- **1 leek**
- **A 5- to 7-pound smoked pork shoulder (also called a picnic)**
- **1 carrot, thinly sliced**
- **1 medium onion, thinly slivered**
- **1 small celery root (½ to ¾ lb), peeled and cut in 2-inch julienne strips**
- **Half a bay leaf**
- **2 cups Alsatian Sylvaner or other dry white wine**
- **2 quarts water**
- **24 small white boiling onions (about 1¼ lbs)**
- **1 tablespoon Dijon mustard**
- **¼ cup whipping cream**
- **Chopped fresh parsley, for garnish**

1. Prepare leek as in recipe for Viennese Simmered Dinner (see page 59).

2. Place meat in a deep 6- to 8-quart kettle. Add leek, carrot, onion, celery root, and bay leaf. Pour in wine and water. Bring to boiling over medium heat, cover, reduce heat, and simmer until meat is very tender when pierced (3 to 3½ hours).

3. Meanwhile, about 30 minutes before meat is done, ladle out 2 cups of the broth. Pour over onions in a 2-quart saucepan. Bring to boiling, reduce heat, and boil gently, uncovered, until onions are tender when pierced with a fork (12 to 15 minutes). Pour off all but about ¼ cup of the cooking liquid. Blend in mustard and cream. Increase heat to medium and cook, stirring, until large, shiny bubbles form and sauce thickens slightly.

4. Remove meat to a board, remove and discard rind, and slice to serve with onions. Sprinkle parsley over sliced meat and onions.

Makes 10 to 12 servings.

Connie's Pork and Chicken Adobo

Pork combines with chicken in equal proportions to make a favorite Filipino dish. Accompany it with rice. Although it is not traditional to serve an *adobo* with plain vegetables, steamed asparagus or tender-crisp edible-pod peas taste good with it.

- **3 pounds chicken breasts and small thighs (about half *each* by weight)**
- **3 pounds lean, boneless pork, cut in 1-inch cubes**
- **2 tablespoons salad oil**
- **6 cloves garlic, minced or pressed**
- **½ cup *each* soy sauce and water**
- **⅓ cup distilled white vinegar**
- **Chopped fresh parsley or thinly sliced green onions, for garnish**

1. Remove skin and bones from chicken breasts; remove skin from thighs (bone as well, if you wish, or use a cleaver to chop thighs in half). Cut boned breasts in halves crosswise.

2. In a large frying pan over medium heat, lightly brown chicken pieces and pork on all sides, about half of each at a time (do not crowd pan), in heated oil. Remove and reserve chicken and pork as they brown. When all meat is out of pan, discard fat.

3. Return meats to pan. Mix in garlic, soy sauce, water, and vinegar. Bring to boiling, cover, reduce heat, and simmer until meats are very tender (40 to 45 minutes).

4. Using a slotted spoon, transfer meats to a warm serving bowl and keep warm. Increase heat to high and boil cooking liquid, stirring occasionally, until reduced by about a third. Pour over meat. Sprinkle with parsley to serve.

Makes 8 to 10 servings.

Baked Lamb Stew with Garlic Toast

Here is an easily assembled lamb stew of French origin—as you might guess from the pungent accompaniment of toast spread with roasted garlic. Serve each diner several cloves to squeeze out onto the toast.

- **3 pounds boneless lamb, well trimmed of fat, cut in large cubes**
- **2 cloves garlic, minced or pressed**
- **1 teaspoon salt**
- **½ teaspoon dried thyme**
- **⅛ teaspoon pepper**
- **2 medium carrots, sliced ½ inch thick**
- **2 medium onions, thinly sliced and separated into rings**
- **½ cup pitted ripe olives**
- **1 bay leaf**
- **2 strips orange peel, *each* about ½ inch by 3 inches**
- **½ cup ham strips, ½ inch thick by 1½ inches long**
- **3 tablespoons butter or margarine**
- **¼ cup brandy**
- **1 can (1 lb) tomatoes**
- **1 tablespoon all-purpose flour**
- **Snipped fresh chives or finely chopped parsley, for garnish**
- **Toasted French bread**
- **Roasted Garlic (recipe follows)**

1. Sprinkle lamb cubes with mixture of garlic, salt, thyme, and pepper. Place half of the lamb in a deep 4- to 5-quart casserole. Add, in layers, carrots; onions; and olives, bay leaf, and orange peel.

2. Cook ham strips in 2 tablespoons of the butter in a small frying pan over medium heat until lightly browned. Stir in brandy, scraping up pan drippings. Spoon ham mixture over vegetables in casserole. Drain tomatoes, reserving liquid; chop tomatoes coarsely and add to casserole. Cover with remaining lamb cubes. Pour in reserved tomato liquid.

3. Cover and bake in a 350°F oven for 1½ hours; stir lightly; then cover again and bake until lamb and vegetables are nearly tender (about 1 hour). Meanwhile, soften remaining 1 tablespoon butter in a small bowl and blend smoothly with flour; set aside.

4. Skim and discard surface fat. Stir butter mixture into lamb; bake, uncovered, until lamb is tender and sauce is thickened (about 20 minutes).

5. Serve sprinkled with chives, accompanied by French bread toast to spread with cloves of roasted garlic.

Makes 6 to 8 servings.

Roasted Garlic Place a whole, unpeeled bulb of garlic in a small baking pan. Bake during last 1 hour that stew is cooking in oven, until center cloves feel soft and buttery. Let cool slightly before serving; then separate quickly into individual cloves.

Oven-Baked Iron-Pot Lamb Stew

No lamb stew could be easier to get under way—the meat is simply layered (with no advance browning) in a cast-iron pot with a variety of vegetables and then baked. This stew comes from the sheep-raising country of California's Mendocino County.

- **2 pounds lean, boneless lamb shoulder, cut in 1-inch cubes**
- **1½ teaspoons salt**
- **½ teaspoon *each* ground allspice and crumbled dried rosemary**
- **¼ teaspoon pepper**
- **1 clove garlic, minced or pressed**
- **1 large onion, quartered, then thinly sliced**
- **4 medium carrots, sliced about ½ inch thick**
- **2 cups coarsely sliced cabbage**
- **3 medium-size new potatoes, sliced (unpeeled) about ¼ inch thick**
- **1 can (8 oz) tomato sauce**
- **1 cup dry white wine**

1. Lightly mix cubed lamb with a mixture of salt, allspice, rosemary, pepper, and garlic.

2. In a deep 3½- to 4-quart cast-iron casserole or Dutch oven, alternate layers of seasoned lamb and each vegetable (in a separate layer) in order given, ending with potatoes on top. Pour on tomato sauce and wine.

3. Cover and bake in a 375°F oven until lamb and vegetables are tender, potatoes are lightly browned, and most of the liquid is absorbed (2½ to 3 hours).

Makes 6 servings.

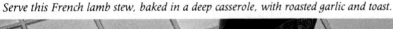

Serve this French lamb stew, baked in a deep casserole, with roasted garlic and toast.

Lamb Stew with Artichokes

Assertively spiced and cooked with red pepper and currants, this generous lamb stew has a sweet-sour flavor suggestive of Sicilian cuisine. Serve it with steamed rice or a pilaf, and green beans.

   4 pounds bone-in lamb neck or shoulder, in large pieces
      Salt and pepper
   3 tablespoons olive oil
   1 large onion, slivered
   1 medium carrot, shredded
   1 stalk celery, thinly sliced
   1 sweet red or green bell pepper, seeded and chopped
   3 cloves garlic, minced or pressed
   ¼ cup dried currants
   ½ teaspoon *each* ground cinnamon and dried oregano
   ¼ teaspoon ground allspice
   1 large can (28 oz) tomatoes
   1 can (6 oz) tomato paste
   1 cup Rich Chicken Broth (see page 9) *or* canned chicken broth
   1 package (9 oz) frozen artichoke hearts
   2 tablespoons lemon juice
      Grated lemon peel and chopped fresh parsley, for garnish

1. Sprinkle lamb lightly with salt and pepper. Brown lamb, about half at a time, in heated oil in a 5- to 6-quart Dutch oven over medium heat. Remove pieces as they brown, and reserve them.

2. Spoon off all but about 2 tablespoons of the drippings. Add onion, carrot, celery, and bell pepper. Cook, stirring often, until onion is soft and begins to brown. Mix in garlic. Return meat to pan. Add currants. Sprinkle with cinnamon, oregano, and allspice. Add tomatoes (coarsely chopped) and their liquid, tomato paste, and broth. Bring to boiling, cover, reduce heat, and simmer until lamb is very tender (about 2 hours).

3. Skim and discard surface fat; then simmer, uncovered, until sauce is thick (20 to 30 minutes). Meanwhile, cook artichokes according to package directions. Drain well and mix lightly into stew. Blend in lemon juice. Taste, and add salt if needed.

4. Serve sprinkled with lemon peel and parsley.

Makes 8 servings.

Spring Lamb Stew with Fresh Peas

Fresh mint seasons the lamb in this glistening stew. Shell fresh peas to be sure it will taste like spring!

   3 pounds boneless lamb leg or shoulder, fat trimmed, cut in 1-inch cubes
      Salt and white pepper
   3 tablespoons butter or margarine
   2 teaspoons salad oil
   3 shallots, finely chopped
   1 clove garlic, minced or pressed
   1 large carrot, sliced about ¼ inch thick
   3 or 4 sprigs fresh mint
   1 cup Rich Chicken Broth (see page 9) *or* canned chicken broth
   1½ cups dry white wine
   1½ to 2 cups shelled fresh peas

1. Sprinkle lamb lightly with salt and pepper. Brown well, about a third at a time, on all sides in 2 tablespoons of the butter and the 2 teaspoons oil in a large, deep frying pan or Dutch oven, removing and reserving lamb as it browns. When all lamb is removed from pan, add shallots, cooking and stirring until they are soft and lightly browned. Mix in garlic and carrot.

2. Return lamb to pan with mint, broth, and wine. Bring to boiling, cover, reduce heat, and simmer until lamb is tender (45 minutes to 1 hour).

3. Remove lamb with a slotted spoon and keep it warm. Strain cooking liquid, discarding carrot and mint. Skim and discard surface fat from liquid. Return liquid to pan and bring to boiling over high heat. Cook, stirring, until slightly reduced and syrupy. Taste, and add salt if needed. Mix in peas and cook and stir until they are tender-crisp (1 to 2 minutes).

4. Cut remaining 1 tablespoon butter in pieces. Off heat, stir in butter, one piece at a time, until melted.

5. Return lamb to sauce, stirring to coat well. Spoon lamb into center of each warm plate. Surround with sauce and peas and serve at once.

Makes 6 to 8 servings.

Some Like It Hot

Chili has become a star. One hears of famous restaurants that fly their special chili around the world to equally famous personages who crave it. Contests are held to select top chili cooks. Whole cookbooks have been written on the subject of chili.

If you are a chili fancier, here are three more recipes to broaden your scope. The first has no beans, but orange, garlic, and tequila flavor it authoritatively. The second, cooked on top of the range, is made with beef and pinto beans and may strike you as the most traditional. The third is an easy oven version with black beans, a combination of pork and beef, and a topping of Monterey jack cheese.

All-Meat Veal Chili

   ½ pound mild Italian sausages
   1 pound ground veal or ground turkey, crumbled
   1 orange
   1 medium onion, finely chopped
   1 sweet red or green bell pepper, seeded and chopped
   1 clove garlic, minced or pressed
   1 teaspoon *each* salt and paprika
   ¾ teaspoon ground cumin
   ⅛ teaspoon ground cloves
   1 small dried hot red chile, crushed
   1 can (1 lb) tomatoes
   ¼ cup tomato paste
   ½ cup tequila
      Sour cream, cilantro (Chinese parsley) sprigs, and avocado slices, for garnish

1. Remove and discard casings from sausages; crumble meat into a large, deep, heavy frying pan. Cook over medium-high heat, stirring often, until lightly browned. Mix in ground veal and cook until it begins to brown. Meanwhile, grate peel and squeeze juice from orange; reserve both.

2. To meats, add onion and bell pepper. Cook over medium heat, stirring often, until onion is soft and lightly browned. Mix in garlic, salt, paprika, cumin, cloves, and chile. Stir in orange peel and juice, tomatoes (coarsely chopped) and their liquid, tomato paste, and tequila. Bring to boiling,

Orange and tequila flavor All-Meat Veal Chili. Serve it from the skillet if you like, dressing up each serving with dollops of sour cream, sliced avocados, and cilantro.

Baked Black Bean Chili

1 cup dried black beans, rinsed and drained

2½ cups water

2 tablespoons all-purpose flour

1 tablespoon paprika

¼ teaspoon cayenne pepper

1½ teaspoons salt

1 teaspoon ground cumin

½ teaspoon dried oregano

1 pound boneless beef stew meat, cut in 1-inch cubes

2 pounds lean boneless pork butt, cut in 1-inch cubes

1 large onion, finely chopped

1 tablespoon lard or soft shortening

2 cloves garlic, minced or pressed

1 can (4 oz) diced green chiles

1 can (1 lb) tomatoes

2 tablespoons tomato paste

Shredded Monterey jack cheese, for garnish

1. Bring beans and water to boiling in a large, heavy saucepan. Boil briskly for 2 minutes; then remove from heat and let stand, covered, for 1 hour.

2. In a large bowl, blend flour, paprika, cayenne, salt, cumin, and oregano. Add cubed meats and mix lightly to coat with flour mixture. Place half of the meat in a deep 4- to 5-quart casserole.

3. In a medium frying pan, cook onion in melted lard over medium heat until soft and beginning to brown. Mix in garlic; spoon over meats in casserole. Add green chiles, beans and water in which they soaked, tomatoes (coarsely chopped) and their liquid, and tomato paste. Top with remaining meat.

4. Cover and bake in a 375°F oven until beef and beans are tender and sauce thickens, stirring once after about 2 hours (3 to 3½ hours in all).

5. Stir well; then taste, and add salt if needed. Serve in bowls; sprinkle with jack cheese to melt into each serving.

Makes 6 to 8 servings.

cover, reduce heat, and simmer until the flavors are richly blended (about 1 hour).

3. If chili seems soupy, uncover and cook over medium-low heat, stirring occasionally, until thickened to your liking. Taste, and add salt if needed.

4. Serve garnished with sour cream, cilantro, and avocado slices.

Makes 4 servings.

Pinto Bean Chili

1 cup dried pinto beans, rinsed and drained

3 cups water

2 pounds boneless beef chuck, fat trimmed, cut in 1-inch cubes

2 tablespoons butter or margarine

1 large onion, finely chopped

1 clove garlic, minced or pressed

2 teaspoons salt

1 teaspoon ground cumin

1 tablespoon chili powder

1 can (1 lb) tomatoes

1 can (4 oz) diced green chiles

1 can (8 oz) tomato sauce

Shredded Cheddar cheese (optional)

1. Bring beans and water to boiling in a large, heavy saucepan; boil briskly for 2 minutes; then remove from heat, cover, and let stand for 1 hour.

2. Brown beef cubes, about half at a time, well on all sides in heated butter in a large, deep frying pan or Dutch oven over medium-high heat, removing and reserving meat as it browns. When all the beef is removed from pan, cook onion in same pan, stirring often, until soft and lightly browned. Return beef to pan. Mix in garlic, beans and their liquid, salt, cumin, chili powder, tomatoes (coarsely chopped) and their liquid, and green chiles.

3. Bring to boiling, cover, reduce heat, and simmer until beef and beans are tender (2 to 2½ hours).

4. Mix in tomato sauce and cook, uncovered, stirring occasionally, until chili is thickened to your taste (about 15 minutes).

5. Serve bowls of hot chili with cheese to sprinkle over, if you wish.

Makes 6 to 8 servings.

Poultry Stews

The versatile chicken is a stewpot favorite. When it is cooked to juicy tenderness in broth, wine, or cream, chicken is a dish that just about everyone likes. And if you have an eye to economical entertaining, look to one of the chicken stews that follows for a dazzling dinner party dish that won't break the budget.

Time was when the chicken that went into the stewpot was a stewing hen—an ample bird of a certain age. These days, however, unless you shop at a special poultry store it's hard to find such flavorful chickens. But you can still achieve rich-tasting chicken stews with the ubiquitous young frying chicken weighing 3 pounds or more. The chicken recipes that follow were all tested with such birds, with seasonings filling in for any flavor failings one might attribute to their youth.

Baked Chicken in Red Wine

When the French serve chicken in wine, or *coq au vin*, it is usually accompanied by boiled potatoes. But why not serve it with baked potatoes? They can go into the oven with the stew for the last 45 minutes to an hour.

> 3 to 3½ pounds meaty chicken pieces (thighs, drumsticks, and breasts)
> ½ teaspoon dried thyme
> ¼ teaspoon *each* dried rosemary and marjoram
> 1 teaspoon salt
> ⅛ teaspoon pepper
> 2 cloves garlic, minced or pressed
> 1 medium onion, thinly slivered
> 1 medium carrot, shredded
> ½ cup julienne ham strips
> 1 bay leaf
> 1½ cups dry red wine
> 3 tablespoons butter or margarine
> ¾ pound large mushrooms, quartered
> 10 small white boiling onions
> ¼ cup brandy
> 2 tablespoons all-purpose flour
> Chopped parsley, for garnish

1. Place chicken pieces in a large bowl. Add thyme, rosemary, mar-

joram, salt, pepper, garlic, onion, carrot, and ham; mix gently. Insert bay leaf in center. Pour wine over chicken mixture. Cover and refrigerate, mixing lightly once or twice, for 8 to 24 hours.

2. Remove chicken from marinade and pat dry, reserving marinade. Melt 2 tablespoons of the butter in a large frying pan and brown chicken pieces well on all sides, about half at a time. As they brown, transfer to a 3½- to 4-quart casserole. Then, in same pan, cook mushrooms and boiling onions, stirring often, until lightly browned. Add to chicken mixture. Stir a little of the wine from marinade into pan to dissolve drippings. Add to chicken; then mix in remaining marinade.

3. In a small, long-handled pan, warm brandy gently over low heat until it is barely warm to the touch. Ignite and pour, flaming, over chicken.

4. Cover casserole and place in a 375°F oven. Bake, stirring lightly once or twice, for 1¼ hours. Meanwhile, soften remaining 1 tablespoon butter in a small bowl and blend smoothly with flour; set aside.

5. Remove casserole from oven. Skim and discard surface fat. Add butter mixture, in bits, to casserole, stirring carefully. Cover again and return to 375°F oven. Bake until chicken is tender and sauce is thickened (about 30 minutes).

6. Sprinkle with parsley to serve.

Makes 6 to 8 servings.

Golden Chicken Stew with Cheese Dumplings

Choose an attractive Dutch oven in which to stew this creamy chicken dish. After the fluffy, cheese-flecked dumplings have steamed atop the bubbling chicken, the stew is served directly from the pot.

> 4½ to 5 pounds meaty chicken pieces (thighs, drumsticks, and breasts)
> Salt, white pepper, ground nutmeg, and paprika
> 2 tablespoons butter or margarine
> 2 shallots, finely chopped (about ¼ cup)
> ½ pound large mushrooms, quartered
> 1 stalk celery, thinly sliced

> 3 medium carrots, sliced about ⅛ inch thick
> ½ teaspoon dried tarragon
> ¼ teaspoon dried thyme
> 2 cups water
> ½ cup *each* dry white wine and whipping cream
> 3 tablespoons cornstarch blended with 3 tablespoons cold water
> ½ cup shelled fresh or frozen peas
> ¼ cup chopped fresh parsley
> Nippy Cheese Dumplings (recipe follows)

1. Sprinkle chicken pieces lightly on all sides with salt, pepper, nutmeg, and paprika. Melt butter over medium heat in a 4½- to 5-quart Dutch oven. Add chicken pieces, about half at a time, and brown lightly on all sides, removing them as they brown.

2. To same pan, add shallots and mushrooms; cook, stirring occasionally, until mushrooms brown lightly. Spoon off and discard as much fat as possible. Mix in celery and carrots. Return chicken pieces to pot. Sprinkle with tarragon and thyme. Add water and wine. Bring to boiling, cover, reduce heat, and simmer until chicken is very tender (1 to 1¼ hours).

3. Remove pot from heat. Remove and reserve chicken pieces. Skim and discard fat from cooking liquid. Blend in cream. Place over medium heat; blend in cornstarch mixture. Cook, stirring, until mixture thickens and boils. Add peas and parsley; then return chicken pieces to sauce. Reduce heat to low.

4. Using 2 tablespoons dipped each time into the sauce, drop dumplings by rounded tablespoons about 1 inch apart over chicken pieces. Cover and simmer until dumplings feel firm when touched lightly (15 to 20 minutes; do not uncover until dumplings have cooked for 15 minutes).

5. Serve directly from Dutch oven.

Makes 6 to 8 servings.

Nippy Cheese Dumplings In a large bowl, stir together 2 cups all-purpose flour, 1 tablespoon baking powder, ½ teaspoon salt, a pinch of ground nutmeg, and ⅓ cup shredded sharp Cheddar cheese. Using 2 forks or a pastry blender, cut in ¼ cup butter or margarine until mixture forms coarse crumbs. Add 1 cup milk *all at once*, stirring just until all ingredients are moistened and a soft dough forms.

Complement *Spiced Orange Chicken* with a fruity white wine, such as a Chenin Blanc or a spicy Gewürztraminer. Rice and peas or green beans complete the menu.

Spiced Orange Chicken

Marinating the chicken first in orange liqueur and fresh orange juice and peel ensures flavor that is as deep as it is delicious.

A 3- to 3½-pound chicken, cut in quarters

½ **teaspoon** *each* **salt and dried tarragon**

¼ **teaspoon** *each* **ground nutmeg, whole cloves, and whole allspice**

1 **clove garlic, minced or pressed**

1 **tablespoon grated orange peel**

1 **tablespoon grated fresh ginger** *or* ½ **teaspoon ground ginger**

1 **cup orange juice**

½ **cup dry white wine**

¼ **cup orange-flavored liqueur**

2 **tablespoons butter or margarine**

1 **tablespoon salad oil**

3 **shallots, thinly slivered (about ⅓ cup)**

½ **cup whipping cream**

1 **tablespoon lemon juice**

Seedless grapes and thinly slivered orange peel, for garnish

1. Place chicken quarters in a large, deep bowl. Add salt, tarragon, nutmeg, cloves, allspice, garlic, grated orange peel, ginger, orange juice, wine, and liqueur. Mix lightly; then cover and refrigerate for 8 to 24 hours.

2. Remove chicken from marinade and pat dry. Strain marinade, discarding seasonings. Melt butter with oil in a large, deep, heavy frying pan or Dutch oven over medium heat. Brown chicken lightly on all sides; as you turn chicken pieces to brown them on last sides, add shallots to pan around chicken.

3. When chicken is browned, pour in marinade. Bring to boiling, cover, reduce heat, and simmer until chicken is tender (about 1 hour). Remove chicken pieces to a warm serving dish and keep warm.

4. Skim and discard surface fat from cooking liquid. Add cream to liquid and bring mixture to boiling over high heat, stirring often. Boil until large, shiny bubbles form and liquid is reduced and slightly thickened. Stir in lemon juice. Taste, and add salt if needed. Pour over chicken.

5. Garnish with grapes and slivered orange peel.

Makes 4 servings.

Chicken in Cider and Cream

Most of France is wine grape country. But Normandy, where this chicken entrée is known as *poulet Vallée d'Auge,* produces apples instead. And so many Norman recipes include cider and/or the apple brandy of the region, Calvados.

A 3½- to 4-pound chicken, cut in quarters

Salt, white pepper, and nutmeg

2 **tablespoons butter or margarine**

1 **tablespoon salad oil**

2 **shallots, thinly slivered (about ¼ cup)**

¾ **pound large mushrooms, quartered**

½ **cup Calvados (French apple brandy) or applejack**

1 **cup French or English hard cider**

1 **cup whipping cream**

Chopped parsley, for garnish

1. Sprinkle chicken quarters on all sides with salt, pepper, and nutmeg. In a large, deep, heavy frying pan or Dutch oven, melt butter with oil over medium heat. Brown chicken pieces well on all sides in butter mixture, removing them as they brown. In same pan, cook shallots and mushrooms, stirring often, until lightly browned. Return chicken to pan.

2. In a small, long-handled pan, warm Calvados gently over low heat until it is barely warm to the touch. Ignite it and pour, flaming, over chicken; stir carefully with a long-handled spoon until flames go out. Add cider. Bring to boiling, cover, reduce heat, and simmer until chicken is very tender (about 1 hour).

3. Remove chicken pieces to a warm, deep serving platter and keep warm. Skim and discard fat from surface of cooking liquid.

4. Stir cream into cooking liquid and bring mixture to boiling over high heat, stirring often. Boil until large, shiny bubbles form and liquid is reduced and slightly thickened. Taste, and add salt if needed. Pour over chicken.

5. Sprinkle with parsley to serve.

Makes 4 servings.

Braised Duckling with Cassis

Chicken is not the only fowl that takes well to cooking in enough liquid to qualify as a stew. This quartered duckling in a fruity brown sauce makes a handsome company dish to serve with thin, crisp French fries or a bulgur wheat pilaf, a green vegetable such as Brussels sprouts, and a full-bodied red wine.

If you buy a frozen ducking, you will have to cut it in quarters yourself. First cut off and discard the wing tips (or reserve them to make broth). Then cut along both sides of the backbone and remove it. Next cut through the breastbone and the wishbone—this gives you two halves; cut each crosswise midway between the drumstick and wing. As you work with the duckling, remove and discard all the surface fat that you can. Quartering the duckling before cooking may sound like trouble, but it is far easier than carving it at the table.

A 4½- to 5-pound duckling, cut in quarters

Salt, white pepper, and ground nutmeg

3 tablespoons butter or margarine

1 tablespoon salad oil

2 cloves garlic, minced or pressed

2 tablespoons cassis (black currant) or raspberry wine vinegar

2 teaspoons tomato paste

¼ cup dried currants

1 cup Rich Chicken Broth (see page 9) *or* canned chicken broth

⅓ cup *each* dry white wine and crème de cassis (black currant liqueur)

1 tablespoon all-purpose flour

1. Sprinkle quartered duckling on all sides with salt, pepper, and nutmeg. Melt 2 tablespoons of the butter with the oil in a large, deep, heavy frying pan over medium heat. Brown duckling well on all sides in butter mixture, removing pieces as they brown.

2. Pour off and discard all but a glazing of the fat in the pan; add garlic, vinegar, and tomato paste, stirring to loosen browned bits from pan. Return duckling to pan. Sprinkle with currants. Add broth, wine, and cassis. Bring to boiling, cover, reduce heat, and simmer until duckling is very tender (about 1 hour).

3. Meanwhile, soften remaining 1 tablespoon butter and mix smoothly with flour in a small bowl. Remove duckling quarters to a deep, oven-proof platter or casserole in a single layer and place, uncovered, in a 400°F oven while completing sauce.

4. Skim and discard surface fat from cooking liquid. Bring to boiling, stirring, over high heat. Blend in butter-and-flour mixture in bits, stirring until sauce thickens. Taste, and add salt if needed. Pour sauce over duckling and serve at once.

Makes 4 servings.

Currants, dried and in the form of cassis vinegar and crème de cassis liqueur, flavor this braised duckling and its gleaming sauce.

Chicken Navarin

Navarin is a French term that, if one sticks to tradition, describes a lamb stew. This version with chicken and colorful vegetables is complemented by a thin, crisp gratin of potatoes.

A 3- to 3½-pound chicken, cut up (reserve giblets for other uses)

Salt, white pepper, and paprika

3 **tablespoons butter or margarine**

1 **tablespoon salad oil**

3 **shallots, finely chopped (about ⅓ cup)**

½ **pound large mushrooms, quartered**

2 **cloves garlic, minced or pressed**

½ **teaspoon** *each* **dry mustard and dried basil**

¼ **teaspoon dried rosemary, crumbled**

8 **small white boiling onions**

1 **large tomato, peeled, seeded, and chopped**

1 **package (12 oz) fresh baby carrots, trimmed**

¾ **cup** *each* **dry white wine and Rich Chicken Broth (see page 9)** *or* **canned chicken broth**

¼ **pound edible-pod peas, ends and strings removed**

1 **bunch (about 6) green onions, trimmed to about 6 inches**

6 **baby artichokes, about 2½ inches or less in diameter (directions for preparing follow)** *or* **1 package (9 oz) frozen artichoke hearts, cooked according to package directions**

1. Sprinkle chicken pieces with salt, pepper, and paprika. In a large, deep, heavy frying pan or Dutch oven, melt 2 tablespoons of the butter with the oil over medium heat. Brown chicken pieces well, about half at a time, in butter mixture, removing them as they brown.

2. When all chicken is browned, pour off all but about 2 tablespoons of the drippings. To pan, add shallots and mushrooms and cook, stirring often, until mushrooms brown lightly. Mix in garlic, dry mustard, basil, rosemary, and boiling onions; then add tomato and carrots. Return chicken to pan. Pour in wine and broth. Bring to boil-

ing, cover, reduce heat, and cook until chicken and carrots are tender (45 minutes to 1 hour).

3. During about the last 5 minutes chicken cooks, place edible-pod peas and green onions on top of chicken pieces to steam until they are bright green and tender-crisp.

4. Using a slotted spoon, remove chicken pieces and vegetables to a warm, deep platter, arranging them attractively. Bring cooking liquid to boiling and cook, stirring, until reduced and beginning to thicken. Remove from heat and add remaining 1 tablespoon butter (cut in small pieces) one piece at a time, stirring after each addition. Taste, and add salt if needed. Add artichokes and mix to coat with sauce; then pour sauce over chicken.

Makes 6 servings.

To prepare artichokes Cut off and discard top third of each artichoke, peel off outer leaves down to pale green inner ones, peel stem, and cut in half lengthwise. As you finish preparing each artichoke, immerse it in a bowl filled with 2 quarts cold water to which 2 tablespoons distilled white vinegar have been added. Put prepared artichokes in 1½ quarts boiling salted water in a 3-quart saucepan; when boiling resumes, cover and boil until artichokes are tender when pierced with a fork (about 15 minutes). Drain well and keep warm until ready to add to sauce.

Poached Stuffed Chicken Gascony

Equating prosperity with "a chicken in every pot" is an older idea than one might think. It goes back to Henri IV, a sixteenth-century French king. What he had in mind was the *poule au pot* of his native Béarn in southwestern France. This version is a contemporary one from neighboring Gascony.

A 3½- to 4-pound chicken

Stuffing (recipe follows)

2 **leeks**

1 **medium onion, slivered**

2 **medium carrots, thinly sliced**

1 **medium turnip, peeled, cut in wedges, and thinly sliced**

1 **stalk celery, thinly sliced on the diagonal**

1 **quart Rich Chicken Broth (see page 9)** *or* **2 cans (14½ oz** *each***) canned chicken broth and ½ cup water**

½ **pound small green beans, whole (with ends snapped off)**

Coarse salt

1. Rinse chicken and pat dry; reserve liver for Stuffing and remaining giblets for other uses. Remove and discard any excess fat. Fill cavity of chicken with Stuffing; then skewer or sew it closed securely. Place stuffed chicken in a 4½- to 5-quart Dutch oven.

2. Prepare leeks as in recipe for Viennese Simmered Dinner (see page 59). Add sliced leeks to chicken with onion, carrots, turnip, celery, and broth. Bring broth to boiling over medium heat; then cover, reduce heat, and simmer until chicken is very tender (about 1½ hours). Remove chicken to a warm, deep platter and keep it warm.

3. To boiling broth, add green beans and cook, uncovered, until they are tender-crisp (8 to 10 minutes). Using a slotted spoon, remove vegetables to a serving bowl (or arrange around chicken on platter). Ladle about ½ cup of the broth over vegetables. (Strain remaining broth and freeze it for other uses.)

4. Carve chicken; serve with Stuffing on deep, rimmed plates with vegetables and broth spooned over. Accompany with coarse salt.

Makes 4 to 6 servings.

Stuffing In food processor, place 6 slices torn French bread (crusts removed) and process until fine crumbs form; transfer to a large bowl. (You should have about 3 cups.) Process ½ cup diced ham and a 1-pound chicken breast (boned and skinned) until they have the consistency of finely ground meat; add to bread. Then, in processor, combine liver reserved from chicken, 2 eggs, 1 clove garlic (minced or pressed), 2 tablespoons lightly packed parsley leaves, ¼ cup whipping cream, ⅛ teaspoon ground nutmeg, ½ teaspoon salt, a pinch of white pepper, and 1 tablespoon Armagnac or brandy; process until smooth. Mix lightly but thoroughly into bread-meat mixture.

Note Any stuffing that does not fit into the chicken can be wrapped in blanched cabbage leaves, using about 3 tablespoons stuffing for each; fasten each roll with a wooden pick. Poach in the broth for 15 minutes, adding rolls 5 to 7 minutes before the green beans.

FESTIVE AND FILLING STEWS

For every dedicated cook there comes a time for a splurge—both in the time and skill needed to accomplish a dinner menu and in the kind and quality of foods that compose it. After all, much of the fun of your carefully nurtured culinary skills comes in sharing them.

This is a menu for such an occasion. It begins with *saumon en rillettes*, a buttery terrine of fresh salmon striped with smoked salmon. Serve it as a first course to spread on thin slices of hot toast. It is delicious with champagne, if you want to go all out.

The main course is a French classic, *poulet en demi-deuil*. It gets its name from the circles of black truffles slipped under the skin before the chicken is poached. Even after cooking, the black discs are visible through the pale, translucent skin. The chicken is bathed in a creamy truffled sauce. The entire production takes only one truffle (canned or fresh), thanks to thin slicing and careful allotment. A California Chardonnay or Fumé Blanc is a good wine choice with this chicken.

A hot, upside-down fruit pie concludes the dinner. A variation of the familiar apple version, it is delicious made with either winter or late-summer pears.

Smoked Salmon Terrine

A ¾-pound salmon fillet

½ cup (¼ lb) butter, softened

2 tablespoons lemon juice

⅛ teaspoon cayenne pepper

¼ to ½ pound sliced smoked salmon, cut in ½-inch-wide strips

Butter lettuce leaves

Lemon and tomato wedges, for garnish

1. Place salmon fillet on a rack over about ½ inch of water in a medium frying pan. Bring water to boiling, cover, reduce heat, and steam salmon until it flakes when tested with a fork (6 to 8 minutes). Remove and discard skin and any bones. Let salmon cool until it is barely warm to the touch.

2. In food processor, combine steamed salmon fillet, butter, lemon juice, and cayenne. Process until smooth and well combined. With plastic blade of processor, mix in smoked salmon strips just until blended through salmon-butter mixture.

3. Spread in a buttered small loaf pan (about 3½ inches by 7½ inches). Cover and refrigerate until firm (several hours or overnight).

4. Loosen terrine with a thin spatula; then turn it out and slice about ½ inch thick. Serve cold, on butter lettuce leaves, garnished with lemon and tomato wedges. Serve with hot, thinly sliced toast.

Makes 10 to 12 first-course servings.

Chicken in Half-Mourning

1 can (25 g) black truffles *or* 1 fresh black truffle, about 1¼ inches in diameter

2 tablespoons Madeira (if using a fresh truffle)

2 whole chickens, 3 to 3½ pounds *each*

1 medium onion, sliced and separated into rings

1 medium carrot, sliced

1 stalk celery, sliced

¼ teaspoon white peppercorns

3 sprigs parsley

1 quart Rich Chicken Broth (see page 9) *or* 2 cans (14½ oz *each*) chicken broth and ½ cup water

3 tablespoons butter or margarine

¼ cup all-purpose flour

½ cup whipping cream

2 tablespoons lemon juice

Salt (optional)

1. If using canned truffles, drain and reserve liquid. Cut 12 thin slices from truffle; finely chop rest of truffle (or truffles) and place in a small bowl with truffle liquid (or Madeira, if using a fresh truffle).

2. Rinse chickens and pat dry; reserve giblets for another use. Remove and discard any excess fat. With two fingers, reach into each chicken from neck end and carefully loosen skin from flesh across breasts and tops of drumsticks. Using 6 truffle slices for each chicken, gently slide truffles under skin across breast and tops of drumsticks. Fasten neck and body cavities of each chicken with a skewer. Place chickens side by side in a deep, heavy Dutch oven just large enough to hold them both.

3. To chickens, add onion, carrot, celery, peppercorns, parsley, and broth. Bring broth to boiling over medium heat; then cover, reduce heat, and simmer until chickens are very tender when thighs are pierced with a fork (about 1½ hours). Remove chickens to a warm, deep platter; cover lightly with foil and keep warm.

4. Strain cooking liquid, discarding vegetables. Skim and discard surface fat. Return liquid to cooking pot and boil over high heat, uncovered, until it is reduced to 2½ cups. Remove from heat.

5. In a 2- to 3-quart saucepan, melt butter over medium heat. Blend in flour, cooking and stirring until bubbly. Remove from heat and gradually blend in the 2½ cups reduced chicken broth. Cook, stirring, until thickened and boiling. Blend in cream and return to boiling, stirring often. Stir in lemon juice and chopped truffles with their liquid (or Madeira). Taste, and add salt if needed.

6. Spoon about a third of the sauce over and around chickens on serving platter; serve remainder in a warm sauceboat. Use poultry scissors to cut chickens into quarters to serve.

Makes 8 servings.

Pear Tarte Tatin

1 tablespoon butter or margarine

1¼ cups sugar

3 tablespoons all-purpose flour

1 teaspoon ground cinnamon

Pinch salt

1 tablespoon lemon juice

4 large pears, peeled, halved, cored, and thinly sliced (about 8 cups slices)

Flaky Pastry (recipe follows)

1. Spread butter over bottom and sides of a 9-inch-round cake pan. In a heavy frying pan, heat 1 cup of the sugar over moderately high heat, tipping and tilting pan so that sugar melts evenly, until it is completely melted and a rich amber color. Pour the caramel syrup into the buttered pan to coat the bottom evenly. Place pan on a rack until caramel hardens.

2. In a small bowl, blend the remaining ¼ cup sugar, the flour, cinnamon, and salt. Mix lemon juice with sliced pears in a large bowl; add flour mixture, mixing lightly to coat slices. Arrange pear slices in caramel-lined pan.

3. Place pastry over pears; trim edge of pastry so that it extends over pan edge by about 1 inch. Fold edge of pastry under, pressing it against inside edge of pan. Slash top in several places to permit steam to escape.

4. Bake on lowest rack of a 450°F oven until pastry is well browned and pears are tender when tested with a fork (40 to 45 minutes).

5. To serve shortly after baking, let pie stand in pan just until juices stop bubbling. Then invert hot pie carefully onto a warm serving plate. Let stand with baking pan in place for about 5 minutes; then remove pan and serve the pie hot. If any caramel remains on pan bottom, place pan over direct medium heat until caramel softens; then use a spatula to spread it over pears. Or, if pie is made ahead, leave it in baking pan on a wire rack for as long as 4 hours, until about 20 minutes before serving. Reheat, uncovered, in baking pan in a 350°F oven for 20 minutes. Then invert onto serving plate and proceed as if the pie had just been baked.

Makes 1 pie (8 servings).

Flaky Pastry In a medium bowl, mix 1 cup all-purpose flour and a pinch of salt. With a pastry blender, cut in ¼ cup firm butter or margarine and 1 tablespoon lard until mixture forms coarse crumbs. Mixing lightly with a fork, gradually blend in 1½ to 2½ tablespoons cold water, stirring just until mixture begins to cling together. Use your hands to form pastry into a flattened ball. Roll out on a floured board or pastry cloth to a 13-inch-diameter round.

If you're a good cook eager to show your skills, consider this menu with truffled poached chickens, salmon terrine, and pear tart.

Braised Chicken in Cream with Asparagus

Emerald spears of fresh spring asparagus share the subtly flavored cream sauce of this elegant chicken dish. Add fluffy rice to complete the main course.

3 to 3½ pounds meaty chicken pieces (thighs, drumsticks, and breasts)

Salt and white pepper

2 tablespoons butter or margarine

½ teaspoon dried savory

Pinch ground cloves

1 teaspoon grated lemon peel

6 green onions, cut in 1-inch pieces (use about 3 inches of top of each)

½ cup *each* dry vermouth and Rich Chicken Broth (see page 9) *or* canned chicken broth

1 cup whipping cream

1 to 1½ pounds asparagus spears

1 egg yolk

2 tablespoons lemon juice

1. Sprinkle chicken on all sides with salt and pepper. Heat the butter in a large, deep, heavy frying pan or Dutch oven over medium heat. Brown chicken pieces, about half at a time, in butter, removing them as they brown. When all chicken is browned, pour off and discard all fat in pan.

2. Return chicken to pan. Sprinkle with savory, cloves, and lemon peel. Add green onions, vermouth, and broth. Bring to boiling, cover, reduce heat, and simmer until chicken is tender (40 to 45 minutes). Remove chicken to a warm serving dish and keep warm.

3. Stir cream into liquid in pan and bring to boiling over high heat. Meanwhile, snap off fibrous ends of asparagus spears; cook, uncovered, in a small amount of boiling salted water in a wide frying pan (or steam on a rack over boiling water) just until bright green and tender-crisp (8 to 10 minutes). Add asparagus to serving dish around chicken.

4. When cream mixture is reduced by about a third, reduce heat to low. Beat egg yolk in a small bowl with lemon juice. Beat in a little of the cream mixture. Then stir egg yolk mixture into cream mixture, stirring constantly, until sauce is slightly thickened. (*Do not boil.*) Taste, and add salt if needed. Pour over chicken and asparagus.

Makes 6 servings.

Chicken with Shallots

The shallot, a member of the same family that includes onions of all sorts, has a taste that is at the same time more pungent and less strident than that of the onion. Poached and then caramelized to buttery sweetness, shallots are the crowning touch for chicken quarters cooked in wine and cream.

A 3- to 3½-pound chicken, cut in quarters

Salt and white pepper

¼ cup butter or margarine

10 shallots

1 cup dry white wine

1 cup whipping cream

1½ tablespoons lemon juice

2 teaspoons sugar

2 tablespoons water

1. Sprinkle chicken lightly with salt and pepper. Brown well on all sides in 2 tablespoons of the butter in a large, deep frying pan over medium heat. When you turn chicken to brown last side, add 2 of the shallots (finely chopped).

2. Add wine, cream, and lemon juice. Bring to boiling, cover, reduce heat, and simmer until chicken is tender (about 40 minutes).

3. Meanwhile, blanch remaining 8 shallots in boiling water for about 1 minute; drain and peel. In a small, heavy pan, combine shallots, remaining 2 tablespoons butter, and sugar. Add the 2 tablespoons water and bring to boiling over high heat, shaking pan and stirring mixture until shallots are coated with an amber caramel sauce. Watch carefully during last stages to prevent sugar mixture from burning or sticking to pan. Remove from heat.

4. Remove chicken quarters to a warm serving plate. Skim and discard fat from cooking liquid if needed. Bring to boiling, stirring over high heat, and reduce slightly. Blend in shallot mixture, pour sauce over chicken, and serve at once.

Makes 4 servings.

Rabbit Stewed with Prunes

Plump prunes are a specialty of the Southwest of France, where this entrée of tender rabbit in a savory red-brown sauce originates.

A 3- to 3½-pound frying rabbit, cut up

Salt, coarsely ground pepper, and all-purpose flour

3 tablespoons butter or margarine

1 tablespoon salad oil

1 medium onion, finely chopped

2 shallots, slivered (about ¼ cup)

1 large clove garlic, minced or pressed

1 large tomato, peeled, seeded, and chopped

½ teaspoon dried rosemary

¼ teaspoon dried thyme

⅛ teaspoon ground allspice

1 cup pitted prunes

½ cup *each* dry red wine and Sturdy Beef Broth (see page 8) *or* canned regular-strength beef broth

1 tablespoon tomato paste

¼ cup Armagnac or brandy

Chopped parsley, for garnish

1. Sprinkle rabbit pieces with salt and pepper; coat lightly with flour. In a large, deep, heavy frying pan, melt 2 tablespoons of the butter with the oil over medium heat. Brown rabbit well on all sides, removing the pieces as they brown.

2. When all rabbit is out of pan, add remaining 1 tablespoon of butter, then onion and shallots. Cook, stirring, until they are soft and lightly browned. Mix in garlic. Return rabbit to pan. Sprinkle with tomato, rosemary, thyme, allspice, and prunes. Add wine, broth, and tomato paste.

3. Bring to boiling, cover, reduce heat, and simmer until rabbit is very tender (1 to 1½ hours). Remove rabbit and prunes to a warm serving dish and keep warm. Add Armagnac to sauce; cook over high heat, stirring often, until sauce is reduced and slightly thickened. Taste, and add salt if needed.

4. Pour sauce over rabbit. Sprinkle with parsley.

Makes 4 to 6 servings.

Fish and Shellfish Stews

The dividing line between fish soups and fish stews is a very thin one. Oyster stew strikes many people as soupy, and many a clam chowder is thick enough to eat with a fork.

The recipes that follow have been chosen to represent the stew genre because they are all so substantial that there can be no question about their status as main dishes—and rather elegant ones, at that.

Fisherman's Wharf Cioppino

This is a gloriously sloppy dish to eat. With the pieces of cracked crab in their shells, there's nothing to do but wade in with both hands—with lots of paper napkins at the ready. Provide shellfish or nut crackers in case the crab needs more cracking.

Accompany cioppino with hot garlic French bread (preferably sourdough) and a red jug wine. The best dessert is fresh fruit and perhaps some crisp cookies.

- ¼ cup olive oil
- 1 large onion, finely chopped
- 1 red or green bell pepper, seeded and chopped
- 3 cloves garlic, minced or pressed
- ½ cup finely chopped fresh parsley
- 1 teaspoon dried basil
- ½ teaspoon dried oregano
- 1 large can (28 oz) Italian plum tomatoes
- 1 can (6 oz) tomato paste
- 2 cups dry white wine
- 1 teaspoon salt
- ¼ teaspoon coarsely ground pepper
- ¾ to 1 pound rock cod fillets, cut in 1-inch squares
- 2 medium Dungeness crabs (about 1½ lbs *each*), cooked, cleaned, and cracked
- 1 pound shrimp, shelled and deveined
- 12 fresh clams in shells, scrubbed

1. In a deep, heavy 5½- to 6-quart kettle or Dutch oven, heat olive oil over medium heat. Add onion and bell pepper. Cook, stirring often, until onion is soft but not browned. Mix in garlic, parsley, basil, and oregano. Stir in tomatoes (coarsely chopped) and their liquid, tomato paste, wine, salt, and pepper.

2. Bring to boiling, cover, reduce heat, and simmer for 1 hour. Uncover and boil gently, stirring occasionally, over medium-low heat until sauce is fairly thick (30 to 35 minutes).

3. Add, in order given, rock cod, crabs, shrimp, and clams. Cover and cook until crab is heated through, shrimp are pink, and clams open (20 to 30 minutes). Discard any clams that do not open. Taste; add salt if needed.

4. Serve hot in large, shallow bowls.

Makes 6 servings.

Poached Fish in Avgolemono

The Greek approach to poached fish involves cooking it with potatoes and then bathing both in a tart lemon sauce, or *avgolemono*.

- 1 medium onion, chopped
- 2 tablespoons olive oil
- 6 medium-size new potatoes (about 2 lbs), peeled or unpeeled
- 1 bay leaf
- 3 sprigs parsley
- ¼ teaspoon black peppercorns
- 1 quart Fish Broth or Rich Chicken Broth (see page 9) *or* canned chicken broth
- 3 large sea bass steaks, ¾ to 1 inch thick (2½ to 3 lbs)
- 3 tablespoons lemon juice
- 2 eggs
- Salt (optional)
- Parsley sprigs and lemon wedges, for garnish

1. In a 4½- to 5-quart kettle, cook onion in olive oil over medium heat until soft but not browned. Add potatoes, bay leaf, the 3 sprigs parsley, peppercorns, and broth. Bring to boiling, cover, reduce heat, and boil gently for 30 minutes.

2. Add sea bass steaks on top of potatoes. As soon as liquid begins to boil again, cover, and reduce heat; simmer until potatoes are tender, and fish is opaque and separates into flakes when tested with a fork (10 to 12 minutes).

3. With a slotted spoon, transfer fish steaks and potatoes to a warm, large, deep platter; cover lightly with foil and keep warm. Strain broth and measure 1 cup. (Freeze remainder and use as Fish Broth.)

4. In a medium bowl, beat lemon juice with eggs until well combined. Return the 1 cup broth to kettle in which fish cooked. Off heat, whisk in egg mixture; then continue whisking over low heat until sauce is just thick enough to coat a metal spoon. (*Do not boil.*) Taste, and add salt if needed.

5. Spoon or pour off any liquid that has accumulated in platter; then pour sauce over fish. Garnish with parsley and lemon and serve at once. Cut each fish steak in half and serve in broad, shallow bowls.

Makes 6 servings.

You can use the tip of a claw to pry out every bit of crabmeat in this luscious cioppino.

Bouillabaisse

This interpretation of the classic French seafood mélange comes from the area around Marseilles. It's a fine kettle of fish steaks and fillets, arrayed on a deep platter after cooking. Each diner serves his choice of fish into a pool of the saffron-scented broth in which all were cooked. A hot pepper mayonnaise, or *rouille*, seasons the fish. Toasted croutons of French bread are also offered.

Complete the menu with a green salad that includes marinated artichoke hearts and tiny black Niçoise olives, and a white Zinfandel or light red wine. Add a tart citrus dessert, such as chilled lemon mousse.

¼ cup olive oil

1 clove garlic, thinly slivered

1½ pounds lingcod steaks

1 can (8 oz) tomato sauce

1 teaspoon grated orange peel

⅛ teaspoon fennel seed, crushed

⅛ teaspoon powdered saffron *or* ¼ teaspoon saffron threads

1 quart Fish Broth (see page 9)

1½ pounds sea bass steaks

1 halibut steak (¾ to 1 lb)

1 pound red snapper fillets

Salt (optional)

Hot Pepper Mayonnaise (recipe follows)

Baguette Croutons (prepare a triple recipe; see page 13)

1. Heat olive oil over medium heat in a 5½- to 6-quart kettle or Dutch oven. Stir in garlic. Add lingcod and brown lightly on both sides, turning carefully. Add tomato sauce, orange peel, fennel seed, and saffron; pour in Fish Broth.

2. Bring slowly to boiling, reduce heat, cover, and simmer for 30 minutes.

3. Add sea bass steaks and halibut. Increase heat to medium-low, cover, and cook without disturbing for 5 minutes. Add red snapper fillets, cover again, and continue cooking until snapper flakes easily when tested with a fork (8 to 10 minutes).

4. Carefully remove fish from broth with a slotted spatula and arrange on a deep, warm platter. Taste broth, and add salt if needed. Ladle broth into large, broad soup bowls and pass fish at the table to add to it. Accompany with Hot Pepper Mayonnaise to season each serving to taste and Baguette Croutons to add with the fish.

Makes 8 to 10 servings.

Hot Pepper Mayonnaise In blender, combine 3 large cloves garlic (minced or pressed), 2 tablespoons lemon juice, ½ teaspoon salt, ¼ teaspoon cayenne pepper, and 2 egg yolks. Cover and turn on blender. *Immediately* begin pouring in mixture of ⅓ cup *each* salad oil and olive oil in a very slow, steady stream. Whirl until all the oil is added and mayonnaise is thick and smooth. Makes about 1 cup.

Elegant Fish Dinner

Asparagus or Broccoli Vinaigrette

Creamy Fish Stew

Fluffy Rice

French Bread   Sweet Butter

Almond Tarts

White Wine   Coffee

A variety of seafood—salmon, sole, snapper, mussels, and shrimp—is combined in the creamy main dish that is the centerpiece of this menu. The stew requires last-minute attention, but much of the preparation can be done ahead so that the ingredients are ready to use: Cook the mussels and reserve the liquid; clean the shrimp; prepare the leeks, shallots, and celery; assemble the salmon-filled sole rolls. Start cooking the rice at about the time you add the fish to the kettle. Both the first course and the baked dessert tarts can be completed in advance.

Although a fine white wine such as a California Chardonnay would be a lovely choice to accompany the fish, you might also enjoy a crisp, blushing white Zinfandel or blanc de Pinot Noir.

Creamy Fish Stew

1 quart (about 1½ lbs) uncooked mussels in shells

2 sprigs parsley

⅛ teaspoon white peppercorns

1½ cups dry white wine

3 leeks

¼ cup butter

3 shallots, finely chopped

1 stalk celery, finely chopped

A ½-pound salmon fillet

6 small sole fillets (about 1 lb)

1 pound snapper fillets, cut crosswise into 1-inch-wide strips

½ pound shrimp, shelled and deveined

½ cup whipping cream

2 egg yolks

Salt (optional)

Chopped parsley and lemon wedges, for garnish

1. Clean mussels and cook with parsley, peppercorns, and wine in a 4- to 5-quart kettle, following directions in recipe for Breton Mussel and Shrimp Soup with Rice (see page 52) through Step 3. You should have about 1 cup cooked mussels. Set mussels aside. Strain the mussel cooking liquid through a dampened cloth and reserve the liquid.

2. Prepare leeks as in the recipe for Viennese Simmered Dinner (see page 59).

3. In a 3½- to 4-quart Dutch oven, melt butter over medium heat. Add leeks, shallots, and celery; cook, stirring often, until vegetables are soft but not browned.

4. Meanwhile, cut salmon fillet into 6 equal pieces. Roll each sole fillet around a piece of salmon. Place rolled sole fillets (with ends on under side to hold rolls together) over vegetables. Add snapper strips and shrimp. Measure 1½ cups of the strained mussel cooking liquid. Pour over fish.

The centerpiece of this dinner is a fish stew, known in France as marmite dieppoise, *with mussels, shrimp, and three kinds of fish.*

5. When liquid begins to boil, cover, reduce heat, and simmer until fish is opaque and shrimp are pink (8 to 10 minutes). With a slotted spoon, transfer sole rolls, snapper strips, and shrimp to a shallow 2-quart casserole; cover them lightly with foil and keep them warm.

6. Add cream to cooking liquid and vegetables. Bring to boiling over high heat and cook, stirring often, until large, shiny bubbles form and liquid is reduced by about half. Remove from heat. Beat egg yolks in a medium bowl; beat in a little of the hot liquid. Blend egg yolk mixture into cream mixture. Add mussels. Stir over low heat until sauce is just thickened. (*Do not boil.*) If liquid has accumulated in the serving dish with the fish, spoon it off and blend it into the sauce. Taste, and add salt if needed. Pour the sauce over the fish.

7. Garnish with parsley and lemon and serve at once.

Makes 6 servings.

Almond Tarts

Cream Cheese Pastry (recipe follows)

2 eggs

1 cup granulated sugar

½ cup firmly packed light brown sugar

¼ teaspoon salt

2 tablespoons butter or margarine, melted

½ teaspoon *each* vanilla and almond extract

1 cup ground almonds

¼ cup sliced almonds

¼ cup apricot preserves

1. Divide pastry into 10 equal portions; press each into bottom and up sides of a 3½-inch tart pan about 1 inch deep.

2. In a large bowl, beat eggs until thick and light colored. Gradually blend in sugars; then blend in salt,

melted butter, vanilla, and almond extract. Mix in ground almonds.

3. Divide filling evenly among pastry-lined pans; sprinkle each with a heaping teaspoon of the sliced almonds.

4. Bake in a 350°F oven until pastry and filling are well browned (25 to 30 minutes). Remove pans to a rack to cool for about 10 minutes. Then carefully slip tarts out of pans and onto the rack.

5. Heat preserves in a small pan, stirring often, until bubbly. Strain to remove bits of fruit. Brush tops of warm tarts with warm apricot glaze.

Makes 10 tarts.

Cream Cheese Pastry In a medium bowl, cream ½ cup (¼ lb) butter or margarine (softened) and 1 small package (3 oz) cream cheese (softened) until light and fluffy. Blend in 1 tablespoon amaretto liqueur or brandy. Gradually add 1¼ cups all-purpose flour, blending until mixture is smooth.

QUICK STEWS FOR FAMILY DINNERS

Calling every recipe in this chapter a stew requires a bit of stretching of the strictest definition of that already flexible sort of dish. But if you are willing to concede that cooking meat—or chicken or seafood—in liquid makes it *something like* a stew, then most of these contenders for the stew designation have passed an important test.

And why quibble over culinary rules when these would-be stews offer such delicious advantages? These are any-night-of-the-week dishes that you can fix for a family dinner without a great deal of thought, advance preparation, or time. Most can be ready for the table in about an hour.

You won't find any tuna-noodle casseroles masquerading as stews in the pages ahead. Indeed, it's safe to say that you could invite a couple of your most discerning friends to a dinner featuring Flank Steak Stifado (page 80), Pork Chops à la Normande (page 88), or Creamy Stuffed Chicken Breasts with Leeks (page 92), and no one would suspect that you had found the recipes in a chapter nominally devoted to quick family dishes.

Menus in this chapter include some enjoyable family feasts such as a creamy meatball stroganoff with moist, chocolatey brownies to serve warm for dessert (pages 82–83) and the Fireside Supper with wine-simmered sausages and a crisp, layered potato casserole on page 87.

Stew in a wok? It's a perfect pan for cooking Gingered Pork Strips (the recipe is on page 88). You can also prepare this colorful dish in a large, heavy frying pan—the utensil of choice for most of the quick-cooking, no-fuss recipes in this chapter.

Stews with Less Expensive Meats

These recipes have been, in large part, created to use less costly meats and other ingredients. You will notice, too, that most yield four (or at most, six) servings. That way you won't need to be concerned about great quantities of leftovers.

Flank Steak Stifado

Stifado is a Greek stew to which most cooks would devote hours. But if made with flank steak, as this speedy stew is, it cooks in minutes. The seasonings consist of sweet-sour accents, spices, oregano, and an abundance of onions.

A last-minute topping of crumbled feta cheese melts over the hot steak strips as you bring the dish to the table. Accompany it with a ring of sesame bread, a green vegetable or carrots, and red wine or retsina.

1 to 1½ pounds flank steak

Salt and pepper

¼ teaspoon *each* ground cinnamon and dried oregano

⅛ teaspoon *each* ground ginger and allspice

2 tablespoons butter or margarine

1 tablespoon salad oil

1 medium onion, thinly slivered

1 large clove garlic, minced or pressed

1 tablespoon *each* brown sugar, tomato paste, and red wine vinegar

½ cup dry red wine

⅓ cup crumbled feta cheese

Chopped fresh parsley, for garnish

1. Cut steak across the grain, slicing on the diagonal (if this is difficult, partially freeze the meat first) to make thin strips about 1 inch wide and 2 inches long. Sprinkle with salt and pepper. In a small bowl, mix cinnamon, oregano, ginger, and allspice; sprinkle mixture evenly over all sides of steak strips.

2. In a large, deep, heavy frying pan, melt butter with oil over medium-high heat. Add steak strips and brown on all sides, a half to a third at a time. (The important thing is not to crowd the pan, so that steak will brown quickly without giving up any moisture.) Remove strips as they brown.

This Flank Steak Stifado is a quick-cooking version of a classic Greek beef stew.

3. When all meat is out of the pan, reduce heat to medium and add onion. Cook, stirring often, until soft and lightly browned. Blend in garlic, then brown sugar, tomato paste, and vinegar. Add wine. Bring to boiling, cover, reduce heat, and cook for 15 minutes.

4. Increase heat to medium, and cook and stir onion mixture, uncovered, until it is slightly reduced and thickened. Mix in beef strips and any juices that collected as the beef stood; turn meat gently, coating with onion mixture, until meat is heated through. Taste, and add salt if needed.

5. Transfer to a warm, shallow casserole, and sprinkle with cheese and parsley. Serve at once.

Makes 4 to 6 servings.

Smothered Skirt Steaks

The skirt steak is a rather obscure bit of beef. It lies inside the rib cage, and there are only two to a carcass. For unique texture and flavor, it is worth searching out. You may have to ask for it, because in many markets, this is "the steak the butcher takes home."

Broiled or sautéed quickly just to the rare stage, it is tender and juicy. For those who prefer steak cooked longer, here is a braised version with mushrooms and other savory embellishments.

4 skirt steaks, about 1 inch thick (about 1½ lbs in all)

Salt, pepper, and paprika

1½ tablespoons butter or margarine

1 tablespoon salad oil

1 medium onion, slivered

QUICK STEWS FOR FAMILY DINNERS

½ pound mushrooms, quartered (leave mushrooms whole if they are small)

1 clove garlic, minced or pressed

2 medium carrots, cut lengthwise in quarters, then thinly sliced

½ teaspoon dried savory

2 teaspoons Dijon mustard

⅓ cup *each* dry red wine and Sturdy Beef Broth (see page 8) *or* canned regular-strength beef broth

2 teaspoons all-purpose flour

Chopped fresh parsley, for garnish

1. Sprinkle steaks on all sides with salt, pepper, and paprika. Place ½ tablespoon of the butter in a small bowl and set aside to soften. In a large, heavy frying pan, melt remaining 1 tablespoon butter with oil over medium-high heat. Add steaks and brown well on all sides. Remove steaks as they brown. Reduce heat to medium.

2. Spoon off and discard all but about 2 tablespoons of the drippings (if necessary). Add onion and mushrooms. Cook, stirring often, until onions are soft, mushrooms brown lightly, and most of the mushroom liquid has cooked away. Mix in garlic, carrots, savory, and mustard.

3. Return steaks to pan. Pour in wine and broth. Bring to boiling, cover, reduce heat, and simmer until steaks and vegetables are tender (30 to 45 minutes). Meanwhile, blend flour smoothly with the reserved ½ tablespoon butter.

4. Remove steaks to a warm platter and keep them warm. Bring cooking liquid to boiling over high heat, stirring often. Add flour mixture, bit by bit, stirring until sauce is thickened. Taste, and add salt if needed. Spoon sauce over steaks.

5. Serve sprinkled with parsley.

Makes 4 servings.

Individual Pot Roasts

When you cook plump beef shanks with such traditional vegetables as carrots, mushrooms, and onions in a rich red-brown sauce, they are transformed into one-to-a-person pot roasts in about two hours' time. All you will need to serve with them is a salad and, if you like, baked potatoes.

4 beef shank slices, about 1 inch thick (about 2½ lbs in all)

Salt, pepper, and all-purpose flour

2 tablespoons butter or margarine

1 tablespoon salad oil

1 large onion, thinly slivered

1 stalk celery, thinly sliced

½ pound mushrooms, quartered (leave whole if small)

2 cloves garlic, minced or pressed

3 medium carrots, cut lengthwise in quarters, then in 2-inch-long sticks

8 small white boiling onions (optional)

1 bay leaf

¼ teaspoon dried thyme

1 can (1 lb) tomatoes

½ cup dry red wine

1 tablespoon all-purpose flour

Chopped fresh parsley, for garnish

1. Sprinkle beef shanks on all sides with salt and pepper; then coat lightly with flour. Place 1 tablespoon of the butter in a small bowl and set aside to soften. Melt remaining butter with oil in a large, deep, heavy frying pan over medium-high heat. Add beef shanks and brown well on all sides, removing them from pan as they brown.

2. To drippings in pan, add slivered onion, celery, and mushrooms. Cook, stirring often, until onion is soft and mushrooms brown lightly. Mix in garlic, carrots, boiling onions (if used), bay leaf, and thyme. Return beef shanks to pan.

3. Add tomatoes (coarsely chopped) and their liquid and wine. Bring to boiling, cover, reduce heat, and simmer until meat is very tender (2 to 2½ hours). Meanwhile, blend the 1 tablespoon flour smoothly with the reserved 1 tablespoon butter.

4. Using a slotted spatula, remove beef shanks and vegetables carefully to a warm serving dish. Skim and discard fat from cooking liquid if necessary. Bring liquid to boiling over high heat, stirring in brown bits from pan. Add flour mixture, a little at a time, stirring until thickened and boiling. Taste, and add salt if needed.

5. Pour sauce over beef shanks and sprinkle with parsley to serve.

Makes 4 servings.

Grandmother's Braised Round Steak

This recipe comes from an Italian grandmother, which at once suggests that the rich, red sauce be served over pasta. Try curly loops or fat tubes to catch the sauce in every swirl.

A 2-pound full-cut round steak (boneless or bone-in), fat trimmed

Salt and pepper

1 tablespoon *each* butter or margarine and olive oil

2 large shallots, finely chopped (about ⅓ cup)

1 medium carrot, finely shredded

1 large clove garlic, minced or pressed

¾ teaspoon dried basil

½ teaspoon dried oregano

¼ teaspoon dried rosemary, crumbled

1 tablespoon Worcestershire sauce

1 can (8 oz) tomato sauce

½ cup dry red wine

Up to ½ cup additional red wine

Chopped fresh parsley, for garnish

1. Lightly sprinkle round steak on both sides with salt and pepper. Melt butter with oil in a large, heavy frying pan over medium-high heat. Add round steak (in one piece) and brown well on both sides.

2. When second side is nearly browned, add shallots and carrot around steak, stirring to brown them lightly. Add garlic, basil, oregano, rosemary, and Worcestershire sauce. Mix in tomato sauce and the ½ cup wine.

3. Bring to boiling, cover, reduce heat, and simmer until round steak is very tender (1¼ to 1½ hours).

4. Remove round steak to a warm platter and keep warm. Skim and discard surface fat from cooking liquid if necessary. Bring sauce to boiling, stirring and adding more wine if it is too thick. Taste, and add salt if needed.

5. Divide round steak into serving pieces. Pour sauce over it and sprinkle with parsley.

Makes 6 servings.

QUICK STEWS FOR FAMILY DINNERS

Lemony Veal and Spinach

This distinctive veal stew is a variation of a recipe Rosemary Hinton Barron teaches at her Kandra Kitchen cooking school on the island of Crete. The stew cooks in just a little more than an hour.

> **2 pounds boneless veal shoulder, cut in 1-inch cubes**
>
> **Salt and white pepper**
>
> **2 to 3 tablespoons olive oil**
>
> **2 medium onions, thinly slivered**
>
> **1½ teaspoons ground cumin**
>
> **1 cup Rich Chicken Broth (see page 9) or canned chicken broth**
>
> **1 bunch (about ¾ lb) spinach**
>
> **1 egg**
>
> **3 tablespoons lemon juice**

1. Sprinkle cubed veal on all sides with salt and pepper. Heat 2 tablespoons of the olive oil in a large, deep, heavy frying pan or Dutch oven over medium heat. Add veal, about half at a time, and brown lightly on all sides. Remove veal as it browns. Add more oil if needed.

2. When all veal is browned, add onions to pan and cook, stirring often, until soft but not browned. Mix in cumin. Return veal to pan. Add broth, bring to boiling, cover, reduce heat, and simmer until veal is tender (1 to 1¼ hours).

3. Meanwhile, remove and discard stems from spinach. (You should have about 6 cups leaves.) Blot moisture from leaves after washing, or dry in a salad spinner. Cut leaves crosswise in 1-inch-wide strips; reserve.

4. When veal is tender, uncover and cook for about 10 minutes to reduce cooking liquid slightly. Stir in spinach. Cook over medium-low heat, stirring occasionally, until spinach is wilted and bright green.

5. Beat egg with lemon juice in a medium bowl. Spoon off about ¼ cup of the veal cooking liquid; whisk hot liquid into egg mixture. Then, off heat, gradually blend egg mixture into veal stew. Return to low heat and cook, stirring gently, until stew is thickened and heated through. (*Do not boil.*) Taste, and add salt if needed. Serve at once.

Makes 6 servings.

Family Favorite Dinner

Creamy Meatball Stroganoff

Noodles

Crispy Coleslaw

Warm Espresso Brownies
with Ice Cream

Milk   Red Jug Wine   Coffee

For this dinner, make the coleslaw first so that it can chill to crisp and blend flavors while you are preparing the meatballs.

If you put the rich, extra-chocolatey brownies into the oven to bake while you are enjoying the main dish, they will be ready to cut and serve warm for dessert.

Creamy Meatball Stroganoff

> **Stroganoff Meatballs (recipe follows)**
>
> **2 tablespoons butter or margarine**
>
> **1 tablespoon salad oil**
>
> **1 medium onion, thinly slivered**
>
> **½ pound mushrooms, sliced**
>
> **1 clove garlic, minced or pressed**
>
> **¼ teaspoon paprika**
>
> **1 teaspoon Worcestershire sauce**
>
> **½ cup Sturdy Beef Broth (see page 8) or canned regular-strength beef broth**
>
> **2 teaspoons cornstarch blended with 1 tablespoon water**
>
> **½ cup sour cream**
>
> **Cooked noodles**
>
> **Chopped fresh parsley, for garnish**

1. Brown meatballs, about half at a time, in a large, heavy frying pan in mixture of butter and oil over medium heat. As meatballs brown, remove them to a shallow pan. When all meatballs are browned, place pan of them (uncovered) in a 250°F oven while you prepare the sauce. Pour off and discard all but about 2 tablespoons of the drippings in the frying pan (if necessary).

2. In the same frying pan, combine onion and mushrooms, stirring until both are lightly browned and most of the mushroom liquid has cooked away. Mix in garlic, paprika, Worcestershire sauce, and broth, stirring to blend in brown bits from pan. Stir in cornstarch mixture, mixing until thickened and smooth.

3. Add meatballs to mushroom sauce, cover, reduce heat, and simmer for 10 minutes. Remove from heat and blend in sour cream, stirring carefully to avoid breaking meatballs. Return to low heat, stirring occasionally, until sauce is heated through. (*Do not boil.*) Taste, and add salt if needed.

4. Serve over noodles; sprinkle with parsley.

Makes 4 to 6 servings.

Stroganoff Meatballs In a large bowl, beat 1 egg with ¼ cup milk. Blend in ¾ cup soft bread crumbs, 1 teaspoon salt, ⅛ teaspoon *each* ground ginger and nutmeg, and 1 teaspoon Worcestershire sauce. Add 1 pound ground lean beef and ½ pound ground lean pork, veal, or turkey. Mix lightly; then shape into 1-inch balls.

Crispy Coleslaw

> **1 small green cabbage (1 to 1¼ lbs), thinly shredded (about 8 cups)**
>
> **1 green or sweet red bell pepper, seeded and thinly slivered**
>
> **½ cup *each* finely chopped fresh parsley and thinly sliced green onions**
>
> **1½ tablespoons sugar**
>
> **1½ teaspoons salt**
>
> **¼ teaspoon dry mustard**
>
> **½ cup distilled white vinegar**
>
> **⅓ cup salad oil**

Meatballs in a creamy sauce with noodles are the centerpiece of a family dinner with coleslaw, homemade brownies, and ice cream.

1. In a large bowl, mix cabbage, bell pepper, parsley, and green onions.

2. For dressing, shake (in a covered jar) or stir together sugar, salt, dry mustard, vinegar, and oil until sugar dissolves.

3. Pour dressing over cabbage mixture; mix lightly. Cover and refrigerate until salad is well chilled and flavors are blended (30 minutes to 3 hours).

Makes 6 servings.

Espresso Brownies

3 squares (3 oz) unsweetened chocolate

½ cup (¼ lb) butter or margarine

1 teaspoon instant coffee powder or granules

⅔ cup all-purpose flour

½ teaspoon baking powder

¼ teaspoon salt

2 eggs

½ cup *each* granulated sugar and firmly packed brown sugar

1 teaspoon vanilla

½ cup chopped walnuts

Powdered sugar, for garnish

1. In a small pan over low heat, combine chocolate, butter, and instant coffee. When butter is melted and chocolate is shiny, stir well to blend together.

2. In a small bowl, stir together flour, baking powder, and salt.

3. In a large bowl, beat eggs until thick; gradually beat in sugars until they are well combined. Blend in chocolate mixture, then vanilla. Gradually stir in flour mixture and mix until all ingredients are well blended. Fold in walnuts.

4. Spread in a greased, lightly floured 8-inch-square pan. Bake in a 350°F oven until the edges begin to pull away from the sides of the pan and the center is nearly set when tested with a wooden pick (25 to 30 minutes; do not overbake).

5. Let cool in pan on a wire rack for a few minutes; then cut into bars. Sift powdered sugar over brownies.

Makes 18 bars.

Veal Breast Braised in Soave

Veal breast is often stuffed whole, then braised in liquid or roasted. It's a memorable entrée, but it takes a long time to get ready and to cook. For a faster way with this moist, appetizing cut of veal, have the meat dealer cut through the veal breastbone in several places so that you can separate the meat into single-rib sections. Accompany the stew with quickly cooked spinach or chard.

A 2½- to 3-pound breast of veal, cut in serving pieces

Salt and white pepper

2 to 4 tablespoons olive oil

1 medium onion, slivered

1 medium carrot, shredded

1 clove garlic, minced or pressed

½ teaspoon dried sage

¾ cup *each* Soave or other dry white wine and Sturdy Beef Broth or Rich Chicken Broth (see pages 8–9) *or* canned broth

¼ cup chopped fresh parsley

1. Sprinkle pieces of veal on all sides with salt and pepper. Heat 2 tablespoons of the oil in a large, heavy frying pan or Dutch oven over moderate heat. Brown veal, about half at a time, on all sides, adding more oil as needed. Remove and reserve pieces as they brown.

2. To same pan, add onion and carrot. Cook, stirring often, until onion is soft and lightly browned. Mix in garlic and sage. Return veal to pan. Pour in Soave and broth.

3. Bring to boiling, cover, reduce heat, and simmer until veal is very tender (about 1½ hours). Remove veal to a serving dish and keep warm.

4. Increase heat to high and bring liquid in pan to boiling, stirring often. Cook until liquid looks syrupy and begins to thicken. Stir in parsley. Add salt if needed. Pour over veal.

Makes 4 servings.

Sweet-and-Sour Veal Stew

A creamy Italian-style risotto accompanies this stew to perfection.

2 pounds boneless veal shoulder, cut in 1-inch cubes

Salt, white pepper, and ground nutmeg

2 tablespoons butter or margarine

1 tablespoon salad oil

Pinch *each* dried thyme and oregano

½ cup Marsala or cream sherry

¼ cup Rich Chicken Broth (see page 9) *or* canned chicken broth

2 tablespoons lemon juice

Italian (flat-leaf) parsley and shredded lemon peel, for garnish

1. Sprinkle cubed veal on all sides with salt, pepper, and nutmeg. Melt butter with oil in a large, deep, heavy frying pan or Dutch oven over medium heat. Add veal, about half at a time, and brown lightly on all sides. Remove veal as it browns.

2. Return veal (and any juices that accumulated) to pan. Sprinkle with thyme and oregano. Add Marsala and broth. Bring to boiling, cover, reduce heat, and simmer until veal is tender (about 45 minutes).

3. Remove veal with a slotted spoon to a warm serving dish and keep warm. Bring cooking liquid to boiling over high heat, stirring often, until it is reduced by about half and looks syrupy. Blend in lemon juice. Taste, and add salt if needed. Pour over veal.

4. Garnish with parsley and lemon peel to serve.

Makes 6 servings.

Lamb Meatball Irish Stew

All the colorful elements you expect in an Irish stew are together in this appetizing and time-saving dish. At the heart of it are ground lamb meatballs. No potatoes are cooked in the stew, but small whole ones—boiled or steamed and buttered—are a fine accompaniment, along with a loaf of Irish soda bread.

2 tablespoons butter or margarine

1 tablespoon salad oil

Lamb Meatballs (recipe follows)

½ pound mushrooms, sliced

1 large onion, finely chopped

1 clove garlic, minced or pressed

¼ teaspoon *each* dried marjoram and savory

⅛ teaspoon ground allspice

3 medium carrots, sliced about ¼ inch thick

2 small turnips, peeled, quartered lengthwise, and sliced about ¼ inch thick

1 cup Sturdy Beef Broth (see page 8) *or* canned regular-strength beef broth

2 teaspoons all-purpose flour

¼ cup shelled fresh or frozen peas

Salt (optional)

1. Place 1 tablespoon of the butter in a small bowl and set aside to soften. Melt remaining butter with oil in a large, deep, heavy frying pan over medium-high heat. Add Lamb Meatballs, about half at a time, and brown on all sides, turning carefully. Remove meatballs from pan as they brown.

2. When all meatballs are browned, pour off all but about 2 tablespoons of the pan drippings (if necessary). Add mushrooms and cook, stirring often, until lightly browned. Add onion and cook until soft. Mix in garlic, marjoram, savory, and allspice.

3. Return meatballs to pan. Add carrots, turnips, and broth. Bring to boiling, cover, reduce heat, and simmer until vegetables are tender (25 to 30 minutes). Meanwhile, mix flour smoothly with the softened 1 tablespoon butter.

4. Using a slotted spoon, remove meatballs and vegetables to a warm serving dish and keep them warm. Skim and discard fat from cooking liquid if necessary; then stir liquid to blend in brown bits from pan. Bring to boiling over medium-high heat. Add flour mixture, a bit at a time, stirring until thickened and boiling. Mix in peas and cook just until heated through. Taste, and add salt if needed. Pour sauce over meatball mixture and serve at once.

Makes 4 to 6 servings.

Lamb Meatballs Beat 1 egg in a medium bowl. Mix in 1 teaspoon salt, a pinch of pepper, 1 tablespoon chopped fresh parsley, and ¼ cup soft bread crumbs. Lightly mix in 1½ pounds ground lamb. Shape into 1-inch meatballs.

In the spirit of the Emerald Isle, bake a loaf of crusty, raisin-studded Irish soda bread to complement this lamb stew. With turnips, carrots, mushrooms, and peas, the stew has all the flavors of the more time-consuming traditional version.

Lamb Chops in Beer

Lamb shoulder chops simmer to tenderness in beer with a variety of vegetables to make a meal-in-one-dish.

- 4 **lamb shoulder chops, ½ to ¾ inch thick (about 2 lbs in all)**
- **Salt, pepper, and ground cloves**
- 3 **tablespoons butter or margarine**
- 1 **large onion, slivered**
- 3 **medium carrots, thinly sliced**
- 1 **large clove garlic, minced or pressed**
- 2 **medium tomatoes, chopped**
- 4 **tablespoons chopped fresh parsley**
- ¼ **teaspoon dried thyme**
- 3 **medium potatoes (1 to 1¼ lbs), each cut lengthwise in 8 wedges**
- 1 **bottle or can (12 oz) beer**
- 1 **tablespoon all-purpose flour**

1. Lightly sprinkle lamb chops on all sides with salt, pepper, and cloves. Reserve 1 tablespoon of the butter in a small bowl. Heat remaining butter over medium-high heat in a large, heavy frying pan. Add lamb chops and brown well on all sides, removing them as they brown. Spoon off all but about 2 tablespoons of the drippings (if necessary).

2. To same pan, add onion; cook, stirring often, until lightly browned. Mix in carrots, garlic, tomatoes, 3 tablespoons of the parsley, and the thyme. Add potatoes.

3. Arrange lamb chops over potatoes. Pour in beer. Bring to boiling, cover, reduce heat, and simmer until lamb chops are tender (40 to 45 minutes). Meanwhile, blend flour smoothly with reserved butter.

4. Remove lamb chops to a warm, deep serving platter. With a slotted spoon, remove carrots and potatoes and spoon them over and around chops. Skim and discard surface fat from cooking liquid. Bring liquid to boiling over high heat, stirring often; cook until reduced by about a fourth. Blend in flour mixture, bit by bit, stirring until sauce thickens and boils. Taste, and add salt if needed. Pour over lamb and vegetables. Sprinkle with the reserved 1 tablespoon parsley to serve.

Makes 4 servings.

Spiced Pork Chops with Rhubarb

At the first rosy blush of spring rhubarb, here is a dish to give a menu a lift. You might accompany the tangy chops with spears of early asparagus to celebrate the season.

- 4 **loin pork chops, ½ to ¾ inch thick (1½ to 2 lbs in all)**
- ½ **teaspoon ground ginger**
- **Salt and white pepper**
- 1 **tablespoon** *each* **butter or margarine and salad oil**
- 2 **cups diced rhubarb**
- 1 **shallot, finely chopped (about 2 tbsp)**
- ¼ **cup firmly packed brown sugar**
- ¼ **teaspoon ground cinnamon**
- ⅛ **teaspoon dried rosemary, crumbled**
- ⅔ **cup dry white wine**
- **Chopped parsley, for garnish**

1. Rub pork chops on all sides with ginger; sprinkle with salt and pepper. In a large, heavy frying pan, melt butter with oil over medium heat. Add chops and brown well on all sides, removing chops from pan as they brown.

2. Spoon off all but about 1 generous tablespoon of the pan drippings; then add rhubarb and shallot and cook, stirring gently, until shallot is lightly browned. Stir in brown sugar. Return chops to pan, spooning some of the rhubarb mixture over them.

3. Sprinkle with cinnamon and rosemary. Add wine. Bring to boiling, cover, reduce heat, and simmer until pork chops are tender (40 to 45 minutes).

4. Remove chops to a warm, deep platter and keep warm. Bring rhubarb mixture to boiling over high heat. Cook and stir until sauce thickens slightly. Taste, and add salt if needed. Pour over chops. Sprinkle with parsley to garnish, and serve at once.

Makes 4 servings.

Fireside Supper

Sausage in Wine Savoyard

Crispy Potato Gratin

Green Salad with Toasted Walnuts

Country French Bread   Butter

Wine-Poached Pears
with Raspberry Sauce

Milk   White Wine   Coffee

From the firesides of the French alpine region of the Savoy comes this warming winter sausage supper. For the main dish choose a large ring of Polish sausage and cut it into chunks to serve, or select plump individual Polish or garlic sausages. Either way, the sausage cooks to juicy perfection with onions, tomatoes, and white wine.

To complement the sausage, bake a crisp gratin of potatoes—quick to assemble if you use your food processor to shred the cheese and slice the potatoes. Winter pears poached in red wine and sauced with a crimson purée of frozen raspberries complete this repast.

Sausage in Wine Savoyard

1¼ to 1½ pounds Polish sausage or garlic sausages

2 tablespoons butter or margarine

2 medium onions, thinly slivered

½ teaspoon dried rosemary, crumbled

3 medium tomatoes, seeded and chopped

1 teaspoon Dijon mustard

½ cup dry white wine

Chopped parsley, for garnish

1. Pierce sausage in several places on all sides with a fork. Melt butter over medium heat in a large, deep, heavy frying pan. Add sausage and brown lightly on one side.

Before a crackling fire, what could be more welcoming than this alpine repast? The main dish is garlic sausage—a large ring or rotund links—cooked in wine. Add a crisp potato casserole, bread, and a green salad punctuated with toasted walnuts. Dessert is pears poached in red wine and served with puréed raspberries.

2. Turn sausage, add onions and rosemary, and continue cooking, stirring often, until onions brown lightly. Add tomatoes, mustard, and wine. Bring to a very gentle boil; then cover, reduce heat, and simmer for about 20 minutes.

3. Remove sausage to a warm platter and keep it warm. Bring tomato mixture to boiling over high heat, stirring until it thickens slightly. Taste, and add salt if needed. Spoon over sausage and sprinkle with parsley.

4. Cut ring of sausage in generous chunks to serve.

Makes 4 servings.

Crispy Potato Gratin

4 medium baking potatoes (1¾ to 2 lbs)

1 clove garlic, split

3 tablespoons butter or margarine

Salt, white pepper, and ground nutmeg

2 cups shredded Gruyère or Swiss cheese

½ cup Sturdy Beef Broth (see page 8) *or* canned regular-strength beef broth

1. Slice potatoes very thinly. (Use food processor with thin slicing blade if possible.) Rub a shallow oval or rectangular 2-quart baking dish with cut sides of the garlic. Then butter dish generously, using about a fourth of the butter.

2. Spread about a third of the potatoes in baking dish; sprinkle lightly with salt, pepper, and nutmeg. Scatter about a third of the cheese over potatoes. Repeat layers with remaining potatoes, seasonings, and cheese, ending with a layer of cheese. Dot top with remaining butter.

3. Heat broth to boiling; then pour slowly over potatoes.

4. Bake, uncovered, in a 400°F oven until potatoes are tender and top is crusty and well browned (45 minutes to 1 hour). Serve very hot.

Makes 4 servings.

Wine-Poached Pears with Raspberry Sauce

1½ cups dry red wine

¾ cup sugar

Half a lemon, thinly sliced

4 firm-ripe medium to large pears, peeled and cored from bottom

1 teaspoon vanilla

Raspberry Sauce (recipe follows)

1. In a deep saucepan large enough to hold all the pears side by side, combine wine, sugar, and lemon slices. Bring wine mixture to a boil, stirring until sugar dissolves.

2. Add pears to boiling wine mixture. Cover, reduce heat, and simmer, turning pears occasionally to cover with wine mixture, until they are tender when pierced with a fork (15 to 20 minutes). Remove from heat, remove and discard lemon slices, blend in vanilla, and let pears cool in wine mixture at room temperature.

3. Serve pears standing upright in shallow dishes, at room temperature or chilled. Spoon Raspberry Sauce over each.

Makes 4 servings.

Raspberry Sauce Slightly thaw half of a 12-ounce package unsweetened frozen raspberries. Place in blender or food processor with 2 tablespoons kirsch and ⅓ cup powdered sugar. Blend or process until smoothly puréed. Strain to remove seeds. Makes about ¾ cup.

Gingered Pork Strips

Purists will insist that this stew by any other reckoning is a stir-fry. Yet the elements of many stews—meat, onions, mushrooms, celery, carrots, seasonings, and liquid—are here, and the method is a brief version of stew cooking techniques. Whatever it is called, it adds up to a colorful dish of tender pork strips to serve over steamed brown rice.

- **1½ to 2 pounds lean boneless pork**
- **2 tablespoons salad oil**
- **1 medium onion, thinly slivered**
- **½ pound mushrooms, thinly sliced**
- **1 clove garlic, minced or pressed**
- **1 stalk celery, thinly sliced on the diagonal**
- **1 medium carrot, thinly sliced on the diagonal**
- **¼ cup *each* dry sherry and Rich Chicken Broth (see page 9) *or* canned chicken broth**
- **2 teaspoons grated fresh ginger *or* ½ teaspoon ground ginger**
- **¼ cup soy sauce**
- **2 tablespoons water**
- **1 teaspoon sugar**
- **2 teaspoons cornstarch**
- **¼ pound edible-pod peas**
- **3 green onions, thinly sliced on the diagonal**

1. Cut pork into thin strips about ¾ inch wide and 2 inches long. Brown strips, about half at a time, in heated oil in a large, heavy frying pan over medium-high heat, removing strips as they brown and reserving them in a shallow dish.

2. To same pan, add onion and mushrooms, cooking and stirring until onion is limp and mushrooms brown lightly. Mix in garlic, celery, and carrot; cook and stir over medium heat for 2 to 3 minutes more. Return browned pork (and any juices) to pan. Mix in sherry, broth, and ginger. Reduce heat, cover, and simmer for 5 minutes.

3. Meanwhile, in a small bowl, blend soy sauce, water, sugar, and cornstarch. Remove the ends and strings from the peas and cut each (unless very small) on the diagonal into 3 pieces. Blend soy sauce mixture into pork and vegetables. Stir in peas and green onions. Cook, uncovered, stirring constantly, over medium-high heat until sauce boils and thickens and peas are just tender and bright green. Serve at once.

Makes 4 to 6 servings.

Pork Chops à la Normande

Here is a temptingly fruity fall or winter dish—pork chops tenderly simmered with apples, cider, and cream. It's good with rice or fluffy homemade mashed potatoes.

- **4 loin pork chops, ½ to ¾ inch thick (1½ to 2 lbs in all)**
- **Salt, white pepper, and nutmeg**
- **2 tablespoons butter or margarine**
- **1 tablespoon salad oil**
- **1 small onion, thinly slivered**
- **2 large tart cooking apples, peeled, quartered, cored, and thinly sliced**
- **½ cup apple cider or apple juice**
- **1 tablespoon Dijon mustard**
- **½ cup whipping cream**
- **Watercress sprigs, for garnish**

1. Sprinkle pork chops on all sides with salt, pepper, and nutmeg. In a large, deep, heavy frying pan, melt butter with oil over medium heat. Add chops and brown well on all sides, removing chops from pan as they brown. Pour off and discard all but about 2 tablespoons of the drippings.

2. To same pan, add onion and apples and cook, stirring gently, until onions are soft and lightly browned. Return chops to pan, spooning apple and onion mixture over them.

3. In a small bowl, blend apple cider with mustard; pour over pork chops. Add cream. Bring to boiling, cover, reduce heat, and simmer until the pork chops are tender (about 40 to 45 minutes).

4. Remove chops with most of the apples and onions to a warm deep platter and keep warm. Bring cooking liquid to boiling over high heat. Cook and stir until large, shiny bubbles form and sauce begins to thicken. Taste, and add salt if needed. Pour over chops. Garnish with watercress and serve at once.

Makes 4 servings.

Bohemian Pork Goulash

Dillseed and caraway seed accent this traditional pork goulash. Noodles are a good foil for the creamy sauce.

- **2 pounds lean boneless pork, cut in ½- by 2-inch strips**
- **Salt and white pepper**
- **1 tablespoon *each* butter or margarine and salad oil**
- **2 medium onions, thinly sliced and separated into rings**
- **1 clove garlic, minced or pressed**
- **1 tablespoon sweet Hungarian paprika**
- **2 teaspoons caraway seed**
- **½ teaspoon dillseed**
- **1 bay leaf**
- **1 cup Sturdy Beef Broth or Rich Chicken Broth (see pages 8–9) *or* canned broth**
- **⅓ cup dry white wine**
- **1½ teaspoons cornstarch blended with 1 tablespoon water**
- **⅔ cup sour cream**
- **Chopped parsley, for garnish**

1. Sprinkle pork strips on all sides with salt and pepper. Melt butter with oil in a large, heavy frying pan over medium-high heat.

2. Add pork strips, about half at a time, and brown well on all sides. Remove pork strips as they brown. When all pork is browned, spoon off all but about 2 tablespoons of the pan drippings (if necessary).

3. Add onions and cook, stirring often, until they are soft and begin to brown. Mix in garlic, paprika, caraway seed, and dillseed. Return pork strips (along with any juices that have accumulated) to pan. Add bay leaf. Pour in broth and wine. Bring to boiling, cover, reduce heat, and simmer until the pork is tender (about 45 to 50 minutes).

4. Remove and discard bay leaf. Blend in the cornstarch mixture, stirring until sauce boils and thickens. Remove pan from heat and blend in sour cream.

5. Return to low heat and stir gently until heated through. (*Do not boil.*) Taste, and add salt if needed. Sprinkle with parsley.

Makes 4 to 6 servings.

Time-Saving Chicken and Seafood Stews

Chicken is not only a dependable money saver, it also wins points for cooking quickly. Divided into parts, it cooks faster still.

If you buy several economical whole birds, you can cut them into serving pieces to freeze and use later in recipes that call for whole legs (thighs attached), breasts, or whatever. Freeze packets of bony pieces and bones you have removed from breasts, as well; then you will have them ready when you want to make Rich Chicken Broth (see page 9).

While fish and seafood are not as easy on the budget as poultry, the tariff is not quite as steep as the price tag might indicate. Consider that fish fillets contain no waste at all—neither fat nor bones—so you can count on more servings per pound than from bone-in poultry. By avoiding glamorous and much-in-demand fish and keeping an eye out for specials, it is often possible to find some truly good buys.

Spices, honey, lemons, and fresh apricots enhance chicken on a bed of brown rice.

Chicken Rosemary with Sherry

Cook this chicken in either a large range-top frying pan or an electric one. The idea is to cook at a temperature that eventually will reduce most of the liquid to a caramel-like glaze for the chicken pieces. If you like, you can cook tiny red potatoes among the chicken pieces; add them just before you cover the pan.

- **A 3- to 3½-pound chicken, cut up (reserve giblets for other uses)**
- **Salt and pepper**
- **2 tablespoons olive oil**
- **1 large shallot, finely chopped (about 2 tbsp)**
- **2 large cloves garlic, minced or pressed**
- **3 sprigs fresh rosemary *or* 1½ teaspoons dried rosemary**
- **¼ cup dry sherry**
- **2 tablespoons lemon juice**
- **Chopped parsley, for garnish**

1. Sprinkle chicken pieces on all sides with salt and pepper.

2. Heat oil in a large, deep, heavy frying pan or electric frying pan over medium heat. Mix in shallot and garlic. Add chicken, skin sides down, to coat with oil mixture. Turn to brown undersides of pieces; then turn and brown skin sides lightly. Without turning chicken again, add rosemary sprigs or sprinkle with rosemary. Pour in sherry.

3. Cover, reduce heat to medium-low, and cook until chicken is tender (40 to 45 minutes). During last 5 minutes, uncover frying pan or open vent of electric frying pan to reduce most of the remaining cooking liquid.

4. Arrange chicken pieces skin sides up on a warm platter. Pour off and discard fat in pan. Add lemon juice, stirring over medium-low heat to blend in caramelized bits from pan. Spoon over chicken. Sprinkle with parsley.

Makes 4 to 6 servings.

Honeyed Chicken with Apricots

If you enjoy chicken combined with fruit, try this dish during apricot season. It's good with brown rice.

- **A 3- to 3½-pound chicken, cut in quarters (reserve giblets for other uses)**
- **Salt and ground allspice**
- **1 tablespoon *each* butter or margarine and salad oil**
- **1 medium onion, thinly slivered**
- **1 small clove garlic, minced or pressed**
- **½ teaspoon *each* ground turmeric and ground ginger**
- **¼ teaspoon ground coriander**
- **1 cinnamon stick (2 to 3 inches)**
- **½ cup water**
- **¼ cup honey**
- **1 lemon, thinly sliced**
- **4 apricots, pitted and cut in quarters**

1. Sprinkle chicken lightly on all sides with salt and allspice. Melt butter with oil in a large, deep frying pan over medium heat. Add chicken and brown well on all sides.

2. When chicken pieces are nearly browned on last sides, spoon off and discard all but a scant 2 tablespoons of the drippings (if necessary). Then add onion and garlic around chicken. Sprinkle with turmeric, ginger, and coriander. Add cinnamon stick between chicken quarters.

3. Add water and honey. Arrange lemon slices in a single layer over chicken. Bring to boiling, cover, reduce heat, and simmer until chicken is tender (45 to 50 minutes).

4. Remove chicken and lemons to a warm, deep serving platter and keep warm. Bring liquid to boiling over high heat, stirring to blend in brown bits from pan, and reduce until syrupy. Add apricots, turning in sauce just long enough to glaze and heat through.

5. Spoon sauce and apricots over chicken.

Makes 4 servings.

Pesto Celebration

Fresh Mushroom Salad

Chicken with Pesto and Walnuts

Garlic-Sautéed Crookneck Squash

Crusty Rolls   Butter

Mrs. Winbigler's Chocolate Pie

Light Red Wine   Coffee

Celebrate fresh basil season with this chicken in creamy green sauce. A salad of mushrooms in a mustard-spiked vinaigrette dressing and an opulent chocolate meringue pie to conclude the dinner are both in keeping with the festive tone.

Fresh Mushroom Salad

Red Wine Vinaigrette Dressing (recipe follows)

1 pound mushrooms, thinly sliced

Butter lettuce leaves

Chopped fresh parsley, for garnish

1. Prepare dressing; shortly before serving, blend again until dressing is well combined.

2. Arrange mushrooms on lettuce leaves in a shallow serving bowl or on individual salad plates. Pour dressing over mushrooms.

3. Sprinkle with parsley to serve. Makes 4 servings.

Red Wine Vinaigrette Dressing In a medium bowl, blend 2 tablespoons red wine vinegar, ½ teaspoon salt, 1 teaspoon Dijon mustard, ⅛ teaspoon white pepper, 1 shallot (finely chopped), and 1 tablespoon chopped fresh parsley. Beating with a fork or whisk, gradually blend in ¼ cup salad oil and 2 tablespoons olive oil until dressing is well combined.

Chicken with Pesto and Walnuts

- **2 tablespoons olive oil**
- **½ cup coarsely chopped walnuts**
- **A 3- to 3½-pound chicken, cut up (reserve giblets for other uses)**
- **Salt and pepper**
- **2 large cloves garlic, minced or pressed**
- **½ cup chopped fresh parsley**
- **1 cup lightly packed fresh basil leaves**
- **⅓ cup dry white wine**
- **1 tablespoon lemon juice**
- **¾ cup whipping cream**
- **Grated Parmesan cheese**

1. In a large, deep, heavy frying pan, heat oil over medium heat. Add walnuts and stir until lightly browned. Remove with a slotted spoon and reserve.

2. Sprinkle chicken with salt and pepper on all sides. Brown in same pan, ending with skin sides up. Discard most of the drippings. Add garlic; half *each* of the parsley and basil; and the wine, lemon juice, and cream.

3. Bring to boiling, cover, reduce heat, and simmer until chicken is tender (40 to 45 minutes). Remove chicken to a warm serving dish and keep it warm.

4. Bring cooking liquid to boiling over high heat. Mix in remaining parsley and basil and half of the walnuts. Transfer to blender and whirl until smooth. Return to pan, taste and add salt if needed, and reheat. Pour over chicken, and sprinkle with remaining walnuts.

For pesto lovers: a chicken-dinner tribute to fresh basil. Walnuts add substance to the sauce in which the chicken cooks.

5. Serve with cheese to sprinkle over each serving to taste.
Makes 4 to 6 servings.

Mrs. Winbigler's Chocolate Pie

- **Chocolate Press-In Pastry (recipe follows)**
- **2¼ cups sugar**
- **¼ cup all-purpose flour**
- **¼ cup unsweetened cocoa**
- **Pinch salt**
- **4 eggs, separated**
- **2 cups milk**
- **2 tablespoons butter or margarine**
- **1 tablespoon vanilla**
- **Pinch cream of tartar**

1. Press Chocolate Press-In Pastry into bottom and up the sides of a 9-inch pie pan. Bake in a 450°F oven until pastry feels firm to the touch and browns lightly (8 to 10 minutes). Let pastry cool in pan on a rack while you prepare the filling.

2. In a heavy 2- to 2½-quart saucepan, stir together 2 cups of the sugar, the flour, cocoa, and salt until they are well combined. Add egg yolks. Then gradually blend in milk, using a whisk. Add butter. Place over direct medium-low heat and cook, *stirring constantly*, until mixture boils and thickens.

3. Remove filling from heat and blend in vanilla. Let cool slightly (15 to 20 minutes). Spread in pastry.

4. Beat the 4 egg whites in a large bowl until frothy; beat in cream of tartar and continue beating until soft peaks form. Gradually add the remaining ¼ cup sugar, beating until mixture is stiff and glossy. Spread meringue lightly over chocolate filling. Bake in a 350°F oven until meringue is a pale golden brown (8 to 10 minutes).

Makes 6 to 8 servings.

Chocolate Press-In Pastry Mix 1 cup all-purpose flour, 2 teaspoons unsweetened cocoa, and 3 tablespoons sugar in a medium bowl until there are no more lumps of cocoa. Cut in ⅓ cup firm butter or margarine until crumbly. Beat 1 egg yolk with ¼ teaspoon vanilla. With a fork, stir egg mixture lightly into flour mixture; then use your hands to press dough into a smooth, flattened ball.

Chicken Legs with Piperade

Piperade is a savory vegetable mélange from France's Southwest. It's usually served with eggs, but here it makes a wonderful sauce and side dish in one for chicken. Add rice to complete the main course.

- **4 whole chicken legs (thighs attached; about 3 lbs in all)**
- **Salt, pepper, and ground cloves**
- **1 orange**
- **2 tablespoons olive oil**
- **1 medium onion, thinly slivered**
- **1 *each* sweet red and green bell pepper, seeded and cut in strips**
- **2 cloves garlic, minced or pressed**
- **¼ teaspoon ground turmeric**
- **½ teaspoon dried basil**
- **1 can (1 lb) tomatoes**
- **¼ cup chopped fresh parsley**
- **1 teaspoon cornstarch, smoothly blended with 2 teaspoons water**

1. Lightly sprinkle chicken legs on all sides with salt, pepper, and cloves. Grate peel and squeeze juice from orange; reserve both.

2. In a large, deep, heavy frying pan, heat oil over medium heat. Add chicken legs and brown well on all sides, removing chicken as it browns. Pour off and discard all but about 2 tablespoons of the drippings.

3. To same pan, add onion and bell pepper strips. Cook, stirring, until onion is soft but not brown. Mix in garlic, turmeric, and basil. Return chicken to pan. Add tomatoes (coarsely chopped) and their liquid, reserved orange juice, about half of the grated orange peel, and half of the parsley.

4. Bring to boiling, cover, reduce heat, and simmer until chicken is tender (about 45 minutes). Remove chicken to a warm serving dish and keep warm. If necessary, skim and discard fat from cooking liquid. Bring to boiling over high heat, stirring until liquid is reduced by about a third. Blend in cornstarch mixture, stirring until thickened and clear. Taste, and add salt if needed.

5. Spoon sauce over chicken. Serve sprinkled with reserved orange peel and chopped parsley.

Makes 4 servings.

Creamy Stuffed Chicken Breasts with Leeks

Although they look like a company dish, these rolled chicken breasts are easy enough to cook after a hard day's work—especially if you've thought ahead and pounded and stuffed the chicken the night before.

3 leeks

2 whole chicken breasts (4 halves, about 2 lbs in all), halved, boned, and skinned

White pepper, nutmeg, and paprika

3 tablespoons chopped fresh parsley

4 thin slices baked ham

1 tablespoon *each* butter or margarine and salad oil

1 clove garlic, minced or pressed

½ cup Rich Chicken Broth (see page 9) *or* canned chicken broth

½ cup whipping cream

1 tablespoon lemon juice

Salt (optional)

1. Prepare leeks as in Step 2 of recipe for Viennese Simmered Dinner (see page 59).

2. Lightly sprinkle chicken breasts on all sides with pepper, nutmeg, and paprika. Place, one at a time, between sheets of plastic wrap and pound with flat side of a mallet until each breast is about ⅛ inch thick.

3. Place pounded chicken breasts, boned sides up, in a single layer. Sprinkle 1 tablespoon of the parsley evenly over the 4 breasts. Then place a slice of ham over each. (Trim edges of ham, if necessary, so that they do not extend beyond the chicken.) Fold sides in, then roll up from one end of each breast to make about 3½-inch-wide rolls. Fasten ends with small skewers or wooden picks.

4. Melt butter with oil in a 10-inch frying pan over medium heat. Add chicken breast rolls and brown quickly on all sides. Mix leeks, garlic, and remaining 2 tablespoons parsley around chicken. Add broth, bring to boiling, cover, reduce heat, and simmer until chicken is cooked through (20 to 25 minutes).

5. Transfer chicken rolls to a warm serving dish and keep warm. To pan, add whipping cream. Cook over high heat, stirring often, until large, shiny bubbles form and liquid is slightly thickened. Mix in lemon juice. Taste, and add salt if needed.

6. Spoon sauce over chicken and serve at once.

Makes 4 servings.

Lemon Chicken Breasts

If you are adept with a wok, it is a perfect utensil to use when you cook this speedy interpretation of a favorite Chinese way with chicken breasts.

3 chicken breasts (6 halves, 2½ to 3 lbs in all), boned and skinned

2 lemons

1 tablespoon *each* butter or margarine and salad oil

1 clove garlic, minced or pressed

⅓ cup Rich Chicken Broth (see page 9) *or* canned chicken broth

2 teaspoons *each* cornstarch and sugar

1 tablespoon *each* soy sauce and water

Salt (optional)

1. Cut chicken breasts crosswise in ½-inch-wide strips. Grate peel from 1 lemon and squeeze juice; reserve both. Cut other lemon in half, squeeze juice from 1 of the halves, and mix juices together. Thinly slice remaining half lemon and reserve the slices for garnish.

2. Brown chicken breast strips, about half at a time, on all sides in heated butter and oil in a large, heavy frying pan, electric frying pan, or wok over medium-high heat. When all chicken is browned, return it to pan and mix in garlic.

3. Add chicken broth and reserved lemon juice. Bring to boiling, cover, reduce heat, and simmer until chicken is just firm and opaque (5 to 6 minutes; do not overcook). Meanwhile, in a small bowl, blend cornstarch smoothly with sugar, soy sauce, and water.

4. Add lemon peel and soy sauce mixture to chicken, bring to boiling over medium-high heat, and stir until thickened and smooth. Taste, and add salt if needed.

5. Garnish with lemon slices.

Makes 4 to 6 servings.

Easy Seafood Supper

Olives   Bread Sticks

Fish Stew with Sherry

Rice with Peas

Fresh Peach Crisp

White Jug Wine   Coffee

Olives and bread sticks make good munching—perhaps with a glass of dry sherry—before this meal. It all goes together quickly, because the fish stew needs very little cooking. While its sauce cooks, put together the peach dessert to bake during the main course.

Serve the stew over steamed rice to which you have added shelled fresh or frozen peas (use about ¼ cup peas to each cup of cooked rice) during the last 5 minutes of cooking.

Fish Stew with Sherry

2 tablespoons *each* butter or margarine and olive oil

1 large onion, finely chopped

1 green pepper, seeded and chopped

1 medium carrot, shredded

1 teaspoon paprika

½ teaspoon *each* salt and dried basil

¼ teaspoon ground turmeric

2 cloves garlic, minced or pressed

2 tablespoons tomato paste

3 medium tomatoes, peeled and chopped

QUICK STEWS FOR FAMILY DINNERS

- **1 cup Fish Broth or Rich Chicken Broth (see page 9)** *or* **canned chicken broth**
- **½ cup dry sherry**
- **1 to 1¼ pounds firm, mild-flavored fish fillets, cut in 1-inch squares**
- **¼ pound tiny peeled, cooked shrimp (optional)**
- **2 tablespoons chopped fresh parsley**
- **Lemon wedges, for garnish**

1. In a large, deep frying pan or 3½- to 4-quart Dutch oven, melt butter with oil over medium heat. Add onion, green pepper, and carrot; cook, stirring often, until onion begins to brown. Mix in paprika, salt, basil, turmeric, garlic, tomato paste, tomatoes, broth, and sherry.

2. Bring to boiling; then boil gently, uncovered, until thick (15 to 20 minutes). Mix in fish and shrimp (if used). Continue cooking until fish is opaque and flakes when tested with a fork (3 to 5 minutes).

3. Mix in parsley. Taste, and add salt if needed. Serve at once with lemon wedges.

Makes 4 servings.

Fresh Peach Crisp

- **4 large peaches (1½ to 2 lbs)**
- **½ cup granulated sugar**
- **2 teaspoons quick-cooking tapioca**
- **½ teaspoon ground cinnamon**
- **⅛ teaspoon ground nutmeg**
- **½ cup all-purpose flour**
- **½ cup firmly packed brown sugar**
- **¼ cup firm butter or margarine**
- **½ cup slivered almonds**
- **Ice cream or whipping cream (optional)**

1. To peel peaches, first dip, one at a time, in boiling water to cover for 30 seconds each. Remove from water; then slip off skins with a small knife. Slice peaches thinly. (You should have 3½ to 4 cups.)

2. In a large bowl, mix granulated sugar, tapioca, cinnamon, and nutmeg. Add peaches and mix lightly. Let peach mixture stand while preparing topping.

3. For topping, blend flour and brown sugar in a medium bowl. Cut

The good ship Mauritania is actually a tureen, and it holds the Fish Stew with Sherry. It is berthed beside a luscious dessert—almond-crusted Fresh Peach Crisp.

in butter until mixture is crumbly. Mix in almonds.

4. Spread peach mixture in a greased shallow 2- to 2½-quart casserole. Cover evenly with topping.

5. Bake, uncovered, in a 350°F oven until peaches are tender and bubbling

and topping is well browned (40 to 45 minutes).

6. Serve warm or at room temperature with ice cream or poured cream if you wish.

Makes 4 to 6 serving.

QUICK STEWS FOR FAMILY DINNERS

Sherried Chicken Livers with Polenta

Polenta can be made ahead and refrigerated overnight so that you can serve it with a rich, red chicken liver sauce in a jiffy as a weeknight supper.

- **3 slices bacon, cut crosswise in ½-inch-wide strips**
- **1 pound chicken livers, cut in halves**
- **Salt and pepper**
- **1 large onion, slivered**
- **¼ pound mushrooms, sliced**
- **1 large clove garlic, minced or pressed**
- **½ teaspoon *each* dried basil and oregano**
- **¼ teaspoon dried savory**
- **1 can (6 oz) tomato paste**
- **¾ cup *each* dry sherry and Rich Chicken Broth (see page 9) *or* canned chicken broth**
- **¼ cup chopped fresh parsley**
- **Polenta (recipe follows)**
- **Grated Parmesan cheese**

1. In a large, heavy frying pan over medium heat, cook bacon in its own drippings until browned; remove with a slotted spoon and drain on paper towels. Sprinkle chicken livers lightly with salt and pepper. Cook livers, about half at a time, in bacon drippings until well browned; remove the chicken livers from the pan as they brown.

2. To pan, add onion and mushrooms; cook, stirring often, until mushrooms brown lightly. Mix in garlic, basil, oregano, and savory. Blend in tomato paste, sherry, and broth.

3. Reduce heat to medium-low, and boil gently, uncovered, stirring occasionally, until sauce is thick (10 to 12 minutes). Return chicken livers (and any liquid that accumulated as they stood) to sauce and cook just until they are heated through (2 to 3 minutes). Taste, and add salt if needed. Sprinkle with parsley and bacon.

4. Spoon chicken livers and sauce over polenta. Serve with Parmesan cheese to add to taste.

Makes 4 servings.

Polenta In a large, deep saucepan over high heat, bring 2 cups water and ¼ teaspoon salt to a rapid boil; using a whisk, gradually stir in ⅔ cup polenta. Reduce heat and boil gently, stirring often to prevent sticking and lumping, until mixture is very thick and pulls away from sides of pan when stirred (10 to 15 minutes). Blend in 1 tablespoon butter or margarine and ¼ cup grated Parmesan cheese. Turn mixture into a well-greased small loaf pan (about 3½ inches by 7½ inches). Cover and refrigerate until firm enough to slice (1 to 2 hours or overnight). Turn loaf of polenta out onto a board and cut in ½-inch-thick slices. Heat 1 tablespoon *each* olive oil and butter or margarine in a large, heavy frying pan over medium-high heat. Add polenta slices and brown lightly on all sides, turning carefully. Serve hot with chicken livers.

Turkey Breast with Mushrooms and Garlic

This quick-cooking main dish will remind you of *scaloppine*, but it's made with reasonably priced turkey breast. That's no reason not to serve it with traditional Italian accompaniments such as buttered tagliarini and steamed chard or spinach.

- **1 to 1¼ pounds boneless turkey breast, sliced about ¼ inch thick**
- **Salt, white pepper, and ground nutmeg**
- **2 tablespoons *each* butter or margarine and olive oil**
- **½ pound mushrooms, sliced**
- **2 shallots, finely chopped (about ¼ cup)**
- **2 cloves garlic, minced or pressed**
- **¼ teaspoon dried sage**
- **3 tablespoons chopped fresh parsley**
- **⅓ cup dry white wine**
- **2 tablespoons lemon juice**

1. Cut turkey breast slices crosswise in about ½-inch-wide strips. Sprinkle lightly on all sides with salt, pepper, and nutmeg.

2. Melt butter with oil in a large, heavy frying pan over medium-high heat. Add turkey breast strips, about a third at a time, and brown well on all sides, removing them as they brown.

3. To pan, add mushrooms and shallots, cooking and stirring until mushrooms brown lightly and most of their liquid has cooked away. Mix in garlic. Sprinkle with sage and 2 tablespoons of the parsley. Add wine.

4. Bring to boiling over high heat, stirring until liquid is reduced and syrupy. Blend in lemon juice; then return turkey strips to pan. Stir to heat through and coat with mushroom sauce.

5. Sprinkle with remaining parsley and serve at once.

Makes 4 servings.

Tomato and Oyster Stew

All it takes is one jar of oysters, but with the addition of pasta shells this stew makes three to four servings. Add crusty bread and a big green salad, then sherbet for dessert.

- **3 slices bacon, cut crosswise in ½-inch-wide strips**
- **1 large onion, finely chopped**
- **2 stalks celery, thinly sliced**
- **2 cloves garlic, minced or pressed**
- **1 jar (10 fl oz) oysters**
- **1 can (8 oz) tomato sauce**
- **½ cup dry white wine**
- **1 cup Fish Broth or Rich Chicken Broth (see page 9) *or* canned chicken broth**
- **⅛ teaspoon *each* white pepper and dried marjoram**
- **¼ cup chopped fresh parsley**
- **⅓ cup small shell-shaped pasta**
- **Salt (optional)**
- **Grated Parmesan cheese**

1. In a large, deep frying pan, cook bacon in its own drippings over medium heat, stirring often, until browned. Drain on paper towels. Pour off and discard all but 2 tablespoons of the drippings.

2. To pan, add onion and celery; cook, stirring often, until soft but not browned. Mix in garlic. Drain oysters, reserving liquid. To onion mixture, add oyster liquid, tomato sauce, wine, broth, pepper, marjoram, and half of the parsley. Bring to boiling, add pasta, cover, reduce heat, and boil gently until pasta is just tender (12 to 15 minutes).

3. Mix in bacon and oysters. Cook, uncovered, just until oysters are firm and edges ruffle (2 to 3 minutes). Taste, and add salt if needed. Mix in remaining parsley.

4. Serve stew in shallow bowls with Parmesan cheese to add to taste.

Makes 3 to 4 servings.

Note: Italicized numbers refer to illustrations.

U.S. Measure and Metric Measure Conversion Chart

		Formulas for Exact Measures			**Rounded Measures for Quick Reference**		
	Symbol	When you know:	Multiply by:	To find:			
Mass	oz	ounces	28.35	grams	1 oz		= 30 g
(Weight)	lb	pounds	0.45	kilograms	4 oz		= 115 g
	g	grams	0.035	ounces	8 oz		= 225 g
	kg	kilograms	2.2	pounds	16 oz	= 1 lb	= 450 g
					32 oz	= 2 lb	= 900 kg
					36 oz	= 2-1/4 lb	= 1000 g (1 kg)
Volume	tsp	teaspoons	5.0	milliliters	1/4 tsp	= 1/24 oz	= 1 ml
	tbsp	tablespoons	15.0	milliliters	1/2 tsp	= 1/12 oz	= 2 ml
	fl oz	fluid ounces	29.57	milliliters	1 tsp	= 1/6 oz	= 5 ml
	c	cups	0.24	liters	1 tbsp	= 1/2 oz	= 15 ml
	pt	pints	0.47	liters	1 c	= 8 oz	= 250 ml
	qt	quarts	0.95	liters	2 c (1 pt)	= 16 oz	= 500 ml
	gal	gallons	3.785	liters	4 c (1 qt)	= 32 oz	= 1 l
	ml	milliliters	0.034	fluid ounces	4 qt (1 gal)	= 128 oz	= 3-3/4 l
Length	in.	inches	2.54	centimeters	3/8 in.	= 1 cm	
	ft	feet	30.48	centimeters	1 in.	= 2.5 cm	
	yd	yards	0.9144	meters	2 in.	= 5 cm	
	mi	miles	1.609	kilometers	2-1/2 in.	= 6.5 cm	
	km	kilometers	0.621	miles	12 in. (1 ft)	= 30 cm	
	m	meters	1.094	yards	1 yd	= 90 cm	
	cm	centimeters	0.39	inches	100 ft	= 30 m	
					1 mi	= 1.6 km	
Temperature	°F	Fahrenheit	5/9 (after subtracting 32)	Celsius	32°F	= 0°C	
					68°F	= 20°C	
	°C	Celsius	9/5 (then add 32)	Fahrenheit	212°F	= 100°C	
Area	in.^{2}	square inches	6.452	square centimeters	1 in.^{2}	= 6.5 cm^2	
	ft^2	square feet	929.0	square centimeters	1 ft^2	= 930 cm^2	
	yd^2	square yards	8361.0	square centimeters	1 yd^2	= 8360 cm^2	
	a	acres	0.4047	hectares	1 a	= 4050 m^2	